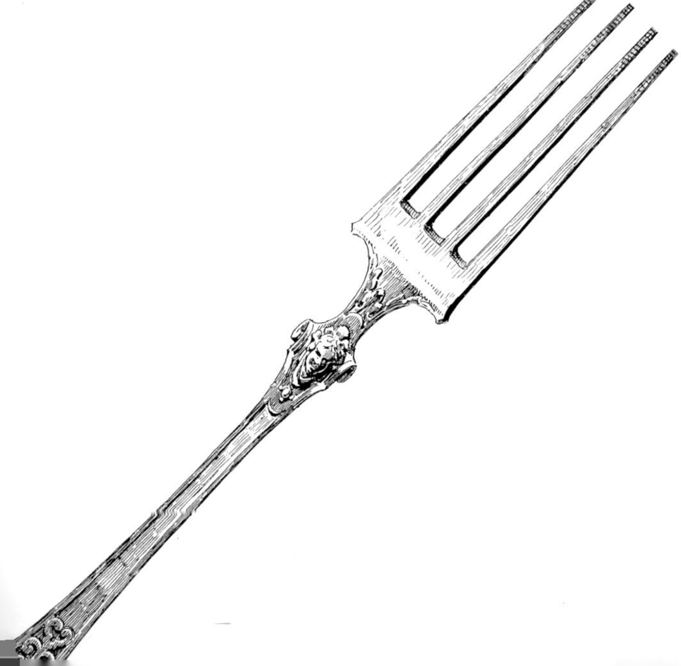

Cooked Books

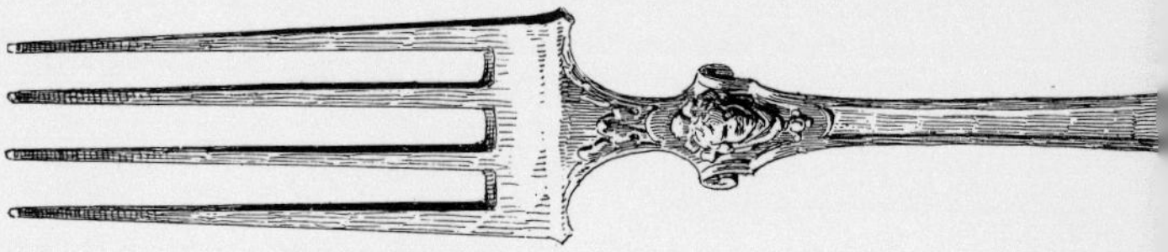

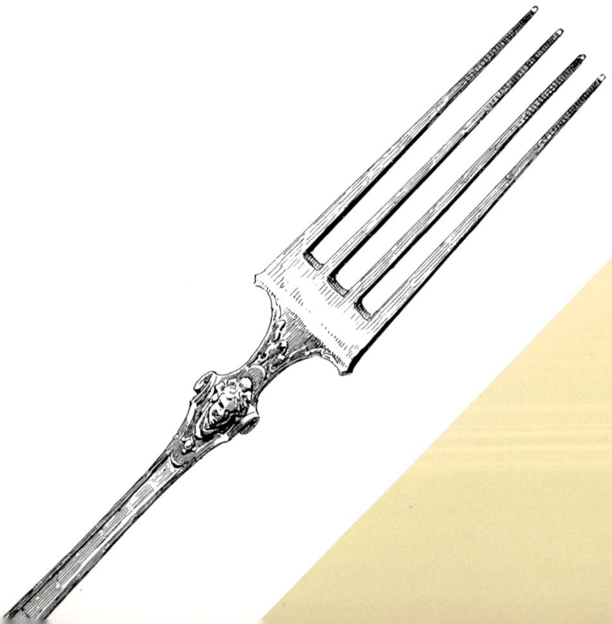

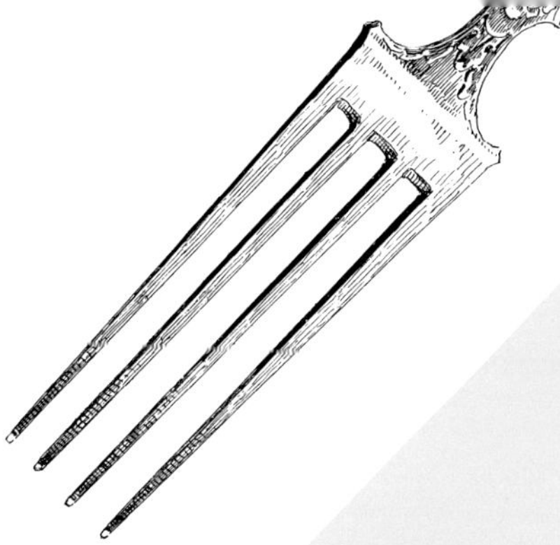

Cooked Books

Recipes from the Staff of Princeton University Press

PRINCETON UNVIVERSITY PRESS | PRINCETON AND OXFORD

Published by Princeton University Press,
41 William Street, Princeton, New Jersey 08540

In the United Kingdom: Princeton University Press,
6 Oxford Street, Woodstock, Oxfordshire OX20 1TW

Library of Congress Cataloging-in-Publication Data
Cooked books / recipes from the staff of Princeton University Press.
p. cm.
Includes index.
ISBN 978-0-691-14149-7 (hardcover : alk. paper)
1. Cookery. 2. Cookery—Humor. I. Princeton University Press.
TX714.C65425 2009
641.5—dc22
2008036250

British Library Cataloging-in-Publication
data is available

This book has been composed in Scala
and Scala Sans

Printed on acid-free paper ∞

PRESS.PRINCETON.EDU

Printed in China
10 9 8 7 6
5 4 3 2 1

The Illustrations

The images of food, tableware, and cooking implements that figure prominently in this book are from *Menu Designs*, published by The Pepin Press, Agile Rabbit Editions, © 1999 and 2005 Pepin Van Roojen, WWW.PEPINPRESS.COM. These images are used with permission. Other incidental images of books and animals are taken from two Dover Electronic Clip Art Publications, *Books, Reading and Writing Illustrations* (CD-Rom and book © 1992) and *1565 Spot Illustrations and Motifs* (CD-Rom and book © 2007) and are used in compliance with terms of use for materials from Dover Publications, Inc.

Assume a can opener.

Contents

Sunday Reading

Main (Dis)Courses I

Beastly Ethics

Main (Dis)Courses II

The Afterlives of Vegetables

Main (Dis)Courses III

Frying Leviathan

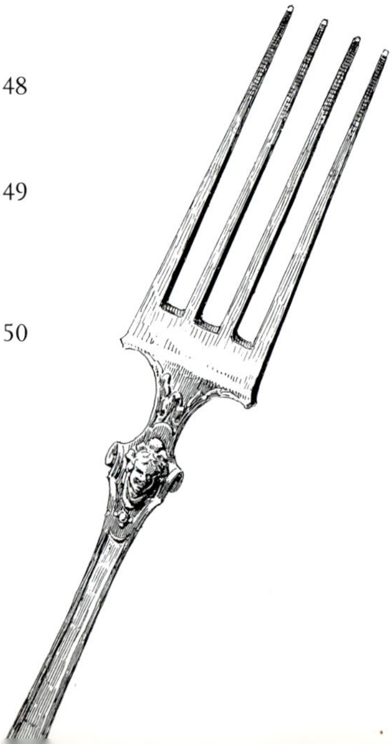

Preface

WITH ALL DUE DEFERENCE TO DOUBLE-DEALING bookkeepers the world over, we are proud to present *Cooked Books: Recipes from the Staff of Princeton University Press.* It includes eighty-two recipes contributed by our colleagues, present and past. In 115 pages, it draws on the best culinary inspiration of our extended publishing community, their families, and their friends. As befits a cookbook, this one covers the full gamut of the meal, soup to nuts. As befits a book publisher's cookbook, it is organized by bibliophilic inspiration: that is, according to the canonical structure of a book: frontmatter for appetizers, text for main dish, epilogue for dessert.

We marry the cultures of cooking and publishing a level deeper by tying the names of many of our favorite dishes to titles of our favorite books and, in some cases, names from the Press's glorious past. And so we have "The Barrington Atlas of of Greek and Roman Chicken," the "Copywriters' Crutch Casserole," and "Scribner's Scrumptious Stuffed-Shell Tacos," to go along with many other distinctive PUP offerings. While the Press-specific epithets may be mysterious to some readers, we trust the quality of the recipes and the liveliness of their presentation will compensate for any confusion.

One recipe in particular stands out as significant: "The Bollingen Martini." This particular concoction is the handiwork of former Press director Herb Bailey, who, along with colleague Joanna Hitchcock, contrived the Bollingen martini as a way of celebrating the Press's famed series. Beyond its delightful contents, this recipe serves as a link not only to our past, but also to the antecedent to this book, *The Princeton University Press Seventy-Fifth Anniversary Cookbook of 1980*. Herb Bailey introduced the previous cookbook with these words:

> It should be said that, unlike our other publications, this cookbook has not been approved by our Editorial Board, a committee composed of faculty members appointed by the President of the University. We believe they would have approved it, but we like to put something over on them once in a while.
>
> We believe that cooking and cookbooks are a legitimate part of scholarly activity. Scholars like to eat, and many do not eat well enough. "Mens sana in corpore sano," we always say. We hope the recipes in this book will nourish thought.

What was true then is true now, and we are honored to stand on the shoulders of our William Street forebears.

I would like to say a special word of thanks to my longtime colleague, fellow editor, and friend Debbie Tegarden who, inspired by the thought of a new Press cookbook, did the sometimes very heavy lifting to orchestrate, organize, and edit *Cooked Books*; to Sarah Stengle, designer *par excellence*, who gave this book its cunning appearance; and to Chief Copywriter Bob Bettendorf and Production Director Neil Litt for steadfast intellectual as well as professional support.

My own experience in publishing books with culinary themes is scant: it is limited to having signed and edited economist Dani Rodrik's 2007 PUP book, *One Economics, Many Recipes*—the "recipes" referring in this case to public policy options for developing countries. So, you see, I have come a long way fast in the craft of cookbook publishing. That said, it is with great pride that I commend to you the fruit of the Press's kitchens. Come and get it!

Peter J. Dougherty
Director
Princeton University Press

Acknowledgments

Eighty-three authors have contributed eighty-two recipes to this book, all of them current or former members of the Princeton University Press staff. Perhaps we should simply extend hearty thanks to one another and leave it at that. Thank you, thank you—eighty-three times over—for taking the time to write up the diverse recipes that made this book possible, pleasing, and (occasionally) peculiar.

We took our inspiration from an earlier Press cookbook, *The Princeton University Press Seventy-Fifth Anniversary Cookbook*, which was assembled and produced by the staff members here in 1980. Twenty-five years later, as Princeton University Press prepared to celebrate its centennial, the idea of pulling together a new staff cookbook seemed like a fine idea. The 2005 observances were, in fact, far more noble and dignified than the modest plan to bring out a commemorative cookbook, and so the new cookbook scheme was temporarily deferred. Nevertheless, Debbie Tegarden, one of the original centennial cookbook proponents, sent out a call for recipes to her colleagues, present and past. The recipes started rolling in, and Tegarden tossed them into a drawer labeled "The One-Hundred-and-First Anniversary Cookbook." Despite the enthusiastic response from so many staffers, as well as the moral and merry support for the project from colleagues Neil Litt and Bob Bettendorf, the cookbook was slow to take shape, and Tegarden soon found herself renaming the bulging recipe drawer "The One-Hundred-and-Second Anniversary Cookbook."

Irma S. Rombauer's first edition of *The Joy of Cooking* begins famously with the universal principle: "Stand facing the stove." Tegarden and Bettendorf met from time to time to sift through the recipes, but they lacked that Rombauerian foundational guidance that could have put them into position to tackle the creation of the printed book. Enter Peter Dougherty, director and man of taste; he pulled the project out of the cold ashes and came up with an innovative vision of the book. And things started to happen. With Peter leading the way, we were joined by the inspirational and indispensable designer, Sarah Stengle; she poured our recipes into her studio cauldron and cooked them up into the frothy, bubbly, and (though we say it ourselves) elegant soufflé of a book you now hold in your hands.

Special thanks are also due to many colleagues who aided in the book's creation: to the magnificent organizational and whip-cracking skills of production coordinator Betsy Litz; to the quiet but timely support of Elizabeth Byrd and Heath Renfroe; and to our production mahatma Neil Litt, who left the porch light on for us during the many months that passed before Peter's initiative and Sarah's genius relit the stove.

FOREWORD

Soups & Appetizers

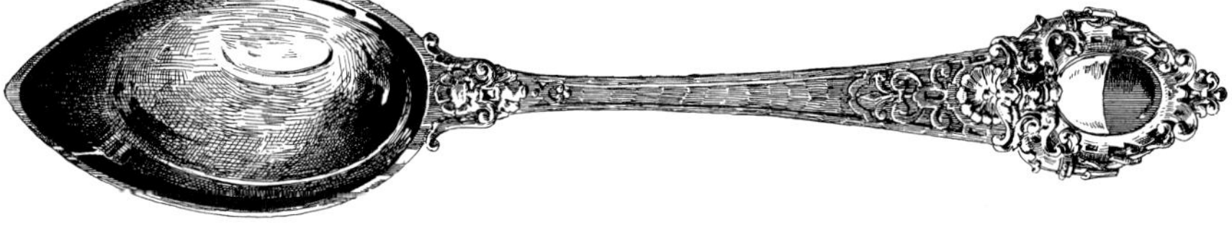

Relatively Easy Stuffed Grape Leaves for Spacetime-Challenged Non-Einsteins

Armenian Dolmas

Alice Calaprice

You don't have to be an Einstein or a stuffed shirt to make these.

¼ cup olive oil (or more if desired)
3 cups chopped onions
1 cup uncooked rice
1½ cups water
1 cup chopped parsley
½ cup raisins
½ cup pine nuts (optional)
1 small can tomato paste, sauce,
  or ½ cup tomato purée
½ teaspoon allspice
½ teaspoon cinnamon
2 teaspoons salt or to taste
½ teaspoon black pepper
jar of grape leaves
spray oil (such as Pam)

Pour oil into a cooking pot; I use a large cast-iron frying pan. Add onions and sauté until golden. Add rice, water, and tomato paste, purée, or sauce. Cover, and cook over a low heat for 30 minutes. Add all the other ingredients, mix together, and continue cooking for about 5 more minutes. Let cool in pan for about 30 minutes.

Open up the rolled grape leaves from the jar and remove stems with a knife if they seem too long. Take about a tablespoonful of the rice mixture and place it in the middle of each grape leaf; close each side of leaf over the mixture. Roll the little package closed. This may take some practice, but it soon becomes second nature.

Now use at least a 2-quart pot to finish cooking the dolmas. You can spread some onions or extra grape leaves on the bottom of the pot to help prevent the dolmas from burning. I usually just use a spray of oil. After you roll each dolma, place it in the bottom of the pot, starting from the edge, to form a circle. Once you have the outside circle complete, start filling in the rest. Then start layering. When you're done, find a plate that fits and invert it over the top of the layers—this will weigh the dolmas down and keep them from unraveling. (The old Armenian ladies do this, but I find that it's really not necessary.)

Pour about 1 to 2 cups of water over the dolmas and cover with a lid. Simmer for about 45 minutes to an hour. Check periodically to make sure nothing is burning. Cool. Refrigerate, but they taste best at room temperature.

This version of dolmas is a bit sweet because of the raisins and spices. Other versions (more oily and salty) can be found prepared in delis, salad bars, or in cans.

The Vanishing Irish

Warm Potato and Leek Soup

Julie Haenisch

2 tablespoons margarine
1 onion, chopped coarsely
4 leeks, white parts only, sliced thin
1 garlic clove, sliced
3 large butter potatoes, peeled and thinly sliced
1 bay leaf
1 tablespoon fresh flat-leaf parsley, chopped
¼ teaspoon dried thyme
4 cups chicken stock
salt and ground pepper
chives, chopped for garnish

Melt margarine in large saucepan. Add onion, leeks, and garlic. Cover and sauté on medium heat for 10 minutes, until soft. Add potatoes, bay leaf, parsley, thyme, and chicken stock. Stir and bring to a boil. Cover and reduce heat to low. Simmer for 20 minutes until potatoes are soft. Uncover, remove from heat, and allow the soup to cool slightly. Purée with a hand blender (or food processor) until smooth. Season with salt and pepper, to taste. Reheat soup over low heat until warm.

Serve hot with artisanal bread for dipping.

Woodstock Winter Warmer

Otherwise Known as Curried Parsnip Soup Rachael Muirhead

1 ounce butter
1 medium onion, finely chopped
1½ pounds parsnips, peeled and diced
1 teaspoon madras curry paste
½ teaspoon cumin
2½ pints chicken stock
juice of ½ lemon
5 ounces cream

Melt butter in large pan; add parsnips and onion, and sauté for 3 minutes. Add curry paste and cumin, and cook for 2 minutes, stirring continuously. Pour in chicken stock and lemon juice, bring to boil, reduce heat, and simmer for 45 minutes. Remove from heat, and allow to cool slightly and liquidize. Transfer to clean pan; reheat gently, adding cream at last minute.

Serve with sprinkling of herbs and paprika. Enjoy!

Recent Hits on Creamy Pumpkin Soup

Andrew DeSio

4 tablespoons butter
1 cup chopped onion
1 clove garlic, crushed
1 teaspoon curry powder
½ teaspoon salt
¼ teaspoon ground coriander
a pinch red pepper flakes
3 cups chicken or vegetable broth
1 16-ounce can pumpkin purée
1 cup half-and-half

Melt butter in a large saucepan over medium-high heat. Sauté onion and garlic in hot butter, stirring continually, until tender—about 2 minutes. Add curry, salt, coriander, and red pepper flakes to onion mixture; mix well. Cook, stirring frequently, for 1 minute. Stir broth into onion mixture. Bring to a boil over medium heat. Cook, stirring frequently, until thickened, 10–15 minutes. Add pumpkin and half-and-half to broth mixture and mix well. Cook for 5 minutes. Pour soup into a blender. Process until creamy.

Serve warm, or reheat to desired temperature. Ladle into soup bowls. Top with green onion curls, if desired.

Preparation time: 12 minutes; cooking time: 23 minutes. Serves 4–6.

Press Release for a Bean Soup with Shrimp

Lisa Fortunato

2 medium onions, chopped
4 cloves garlic, minced
2 medium tomatoes, peeled and cut into wedges
3 (14½–ounce) cans chicken broth, divided
3 cups cooked dried black beans or 2 (15-ounce)
    cans black beans, rinsed, drained
1 teaspoon ground cumin
1 teaspoon oregano
1 teaspoon thyme
1 bay leaf
8 ounces peeled, deveined shrimp (not frozen)
salt and pepper, to taste
cilantro, chopped finely for garnish

Sauté onions and garlic over medium flame until tender (about 5 minutes). Process onion mixture, tomatoes, and 1 can of the chicken broth until smooth; return mixture to saucepan. Add remaining 2 cans of chicken broth, black beans, and herbs to saucepan; heat to boiling. Reduce heat and simmer, uncovered, for 10 minutes. Add shrimp during last 5 minutes. Discard bay leaf and season to taste with salt and pepper.

Serve in soup bowls, sprinkle with cilantro.
Serves 3 (about 1½ cups each).

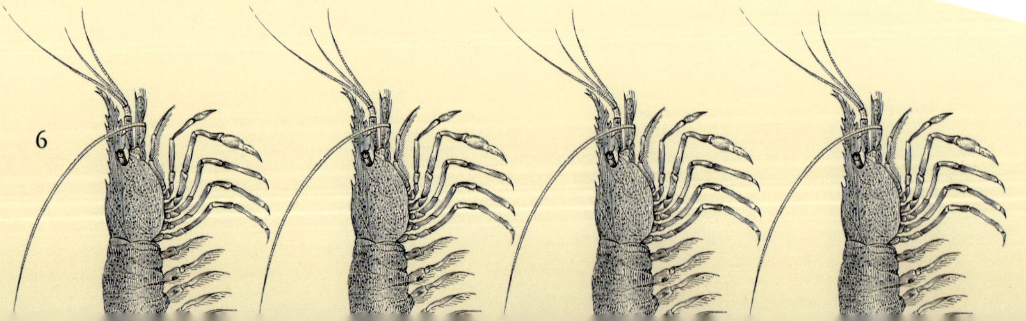

Rethinking Caponata Platter, from Classical Antiquity to Foucault

Clara Platter

From the Platters, Charles and Clara.

1 large or 2 small eggplants (peeled, if you prefer)
½–¾ cup olive oil
6 cloves garlic (or to taste)
¼ cup tomato paste
salt
1 teaspoon crushed red pepper flakes
grated Parmesan cheese
½ cup chopped parsley
1 teaspoon salt (or to taste)

Preheat oven to 375 degrees (F).

Cut eggplant into 1 1½ inch cubes. Put ½ cup olive oil into a greased baking pan with at least 2" sides. Dice garlic; place garlic and eggplant into baking pan. Mix, to get everything covered with olive oil. Cover pan; use foil or something not flammable!

Place eggplant-garlic mixture in oven, remixing with a sturdy metal spoon after 15 minutes to make sure stuff is not sticking to the bottom of the pan. Add more olive oil if necessary: the eggplant will suck up olive oil like crazy at first, but then—as it softens— the oil will return to the pan. So make sure the pan has enough oil to avoid sticking—but be judicious, so you don't end up with too much oil at the end.

After eggplant mixture has begun to soften (30 minutes or so) and the oil has begun to free up, add a ¼ cup tomato paste and stir the mixture thoroughly so paste is evenly distributed. Add 1 teaspoon salt; however, if you decide to garnish the dish with grated Parmesan, cut back on the salt. Add 1 teaspoon crushed red pepper flakes. Continue roasting another 20 minutes or so, or until the eggplant is easily mashed with a fork. Check for spiciness and re-season as necessary.

Add parsley; then add ½ cup grated Parmesan, if you're making a dip. If you want to use as a crostini spread, sprinkle the cheese on top before throwing the mixture under the broiler to brown.

The dish is good to go at this point—hot, cold, or at room temperature. Serves enough to take to parties. Never any leftovers.

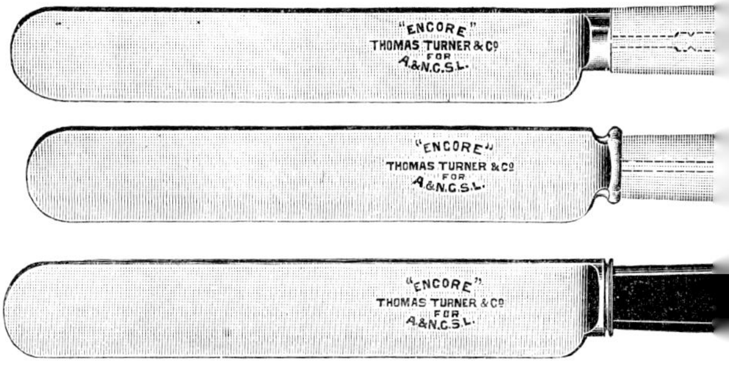

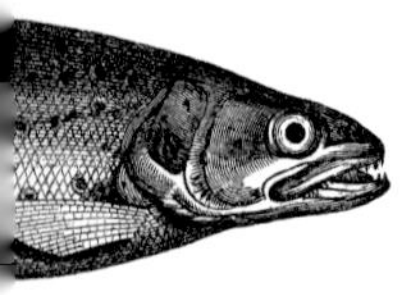

Measureless Fish Soup

Sarah Stengle

This is a recipe I learned as an exchange student in Finland. It is fast to make and very forgiving. It is also pretty to look at—white with pink and green.

Ingredients Are Per Person
1 or 2 waxy boiling potatoes
¼ pound fresh salmon (or any mild white fish)
fish stock—enough to cover the potatoes
milk, to taste
¼ cup chopped onion
butter, just enough to sauté onions
fresh dill, lots of it
fresh chives—optional
dash of allspice
salt and pepper to taste

A Note on the Ingredients

Dill: Fresh dill is essential; don't even bother to make the soup with dried dill. There is no such thing as too much fresh dill.

Potatoes: The waxier the potatoes, the better. Idaho potatoes ruin the soup.

Fish Stock: I like to use hon-dashi, which is available from Oriental grocers. Dashi has a very clean flavor. This soup also tastes good made with water.

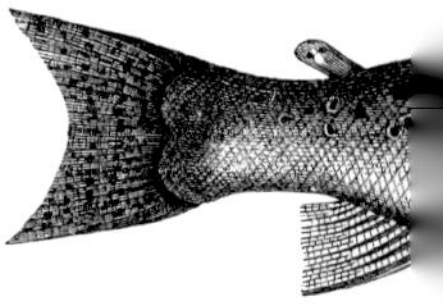

Milk: Anything from skim milk to cream will do fine. I prefer to use skim. Use about the same amount of milk as the fish stock, but the proportion hardly matters.

Butter or Oil: Vegetable oil can be substituted for butter, but do not use olive oil.

Chop the onions finely. Dice the potatoes into ½-inch cubes, or slice as you prefer. Cut the fish into 1-inch cubes. In a heavy pot, sauté the onions until they turn translucent. Add the sliced potatoes and allspice. Add enough fish stock or water to cover the potatoes. Simmer until the potatoes are done, but not overdone, about ten minutes. Add the fish and cook for a scant 3 to 4 minutes more. Add the milk and heat until warm, but do not allow soup to boil. Boiling will curdle the milk. Remove the dill leaves from the stalks and chop together with the chives. Toss the dill into the soup just before serving. Add salt and pepper to taste.

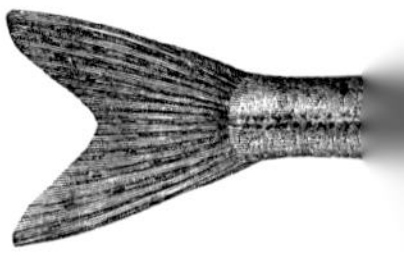

Sunday Reading

Brunch

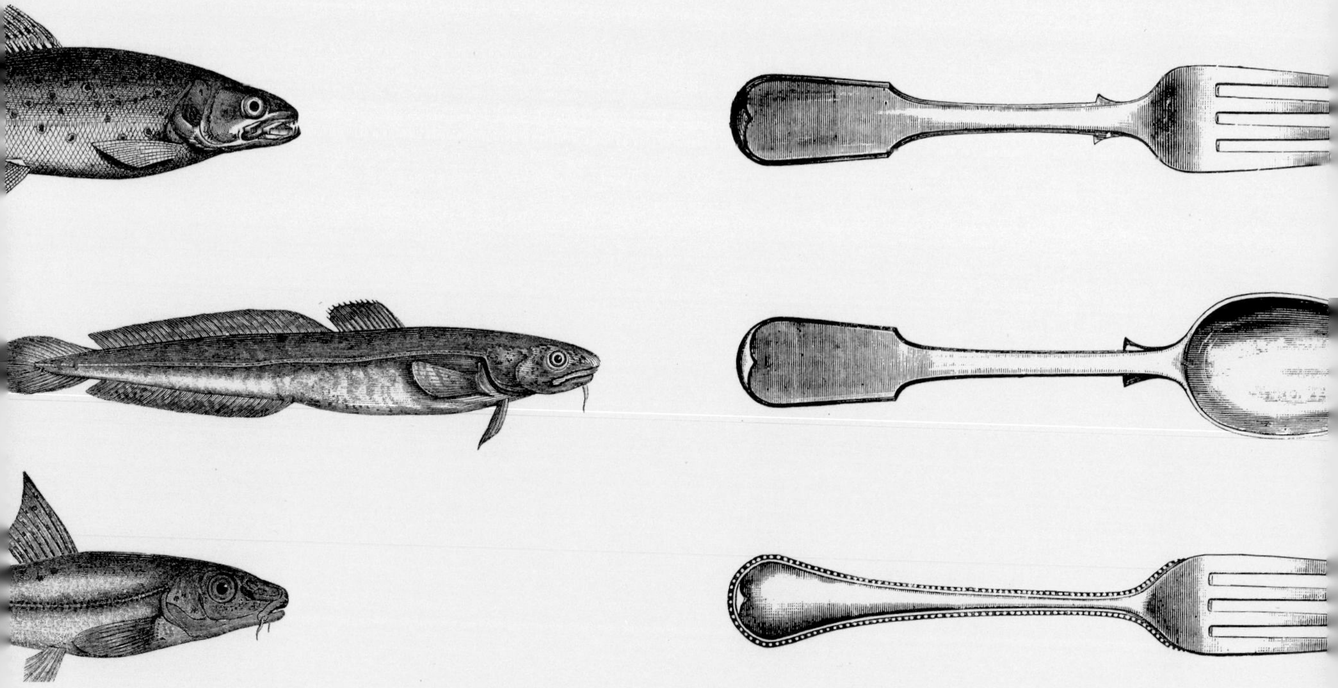

Copywriters' Crutch Casserole

Or Baked Cheese Grits

Bob Bettendorf

Most non-Southerners believe grits are disgusting. So something called "baked cheese grits" must be doubly so, right? Not so, boldly asserts Bob Bettendorf, the world's leading fake Southerner and grits authority. With his magisterial, pathbreaking, incisive, penetrating, compelling, beautifully illustrated, timely, controversial, provocative, previously unknown, unprecedented, comprehensive, elegantly written, far-reaching, sweeping, pioneering, unique, revealing, forthright, readable, landmark, and scholarly-yet-accessible recipe Copywriter's Crutch Casserole, Bettendorf persuasively demonstrates that grits are not only edible, but also consumable. Based on original archival research, cutting-edge laboratory work, firsthand field study, industrial espionage, and hours of sitting in the dark thinking hard, this recipe—the first grits recipe ever published in New Jersey (or in standard English)—will change forever the way three or four people look at the humble corn staple.

1 cup of good quality stone-ground yellow grits
(Not processed white grits.You may be able to find good grits at better gourmet stores or online: copywriters can usually tell you where to look.)
3 cups water
½–1 stick butter (you decide)
½ cup milk or cream
2 teaspoons salt (less any salt you use when cooking grits)
a dash of pepper
⅔ cup grated Parmesan cheese
⅔ cup grated Gruyère cheese
3 eggs

Prepare grits as directed on bag (for some brands, this may mean bringing 1 cup of grits and 3 cups of water to a boil and then simmering them for 30–60 minutes, stirring occasionally. You may add a pat or two of butter and a few dashes of salt.) Pour hot grits into a bowl and stir in all other ingredients. Pour mixture into a 9 x 13-inch pan or casserole dish.

Bake for 45–60 minutes at 350 degrees (F) or until it doesn't jiggle too much. It can jiggle a bit because it will set more as it cools.

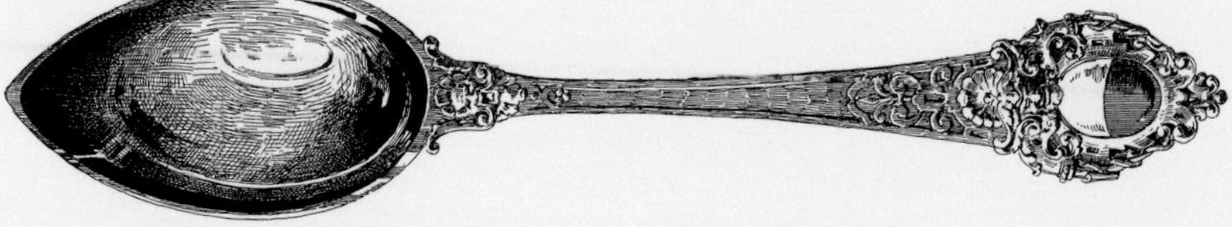

Highly recommended: Reheat refrigerated leftover squares by frying them in butter, in a cast-iron skillet.

Even more highly recommended: Take a refrigerated square (about 4 x 4 inches), cut out a circle in the middle using an upside-down drinking glass with a diameter of about 1½ inches: start frying square in a buttered skillet, and then crack an egg in the circle, flipping several times as it fries.

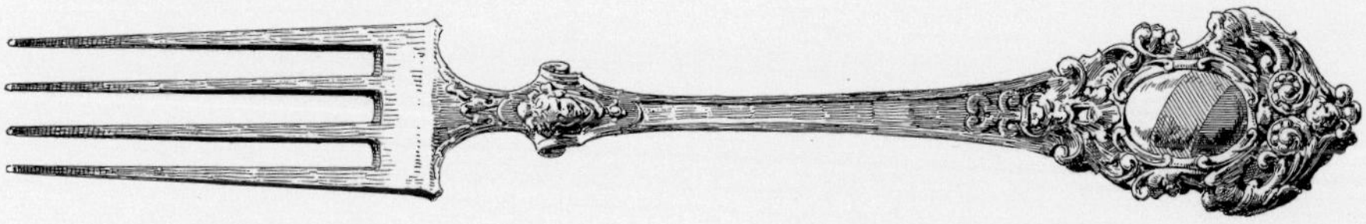

GRITS / CHEESE / BUTTER

Bob Bettendorf holds the Jimmy Carter Chair in Grits Technology at Emory University. He is the author of *Grits: What the Hell Are They?* and *Kiss My Grits: A Grits Lover's Companion to Sitcoms.*

Princeton Annals of Disgusting-Sounding Regional Dishes

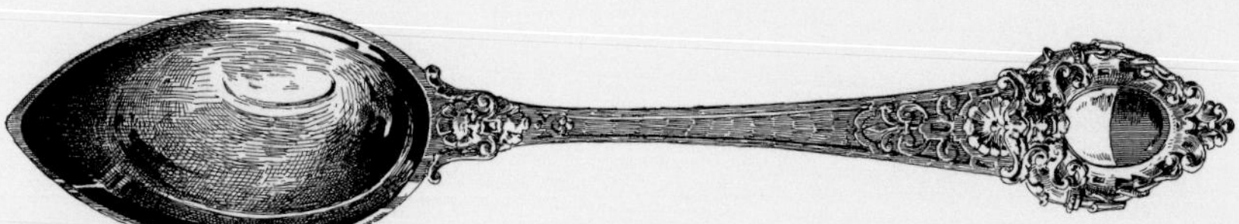

Eggs Iago with Greenblatt Sauce

Steven C. Ballinger

MEMORANDUM:

Subject: Eggs Iago with Greenblatt Sauce

To: Ms. Deborah Tegarden

From: Steven C. Ballinger

Date: February 20, 2008

> To Greenblatt, [author of *Hamlet in Purgatory*] the character of Iago offers the ultimate portrait of the Machiavellian man without qualities, who finds his perfect embodiment in the famous....
>
> —*Jürgen Pieters,* Moments of Negotiation: The New Historicism of Stephen Greenblatt

Dear Ms. Tegarden,

It has come to our attention that there is interest at your institution of higher learning in a better understanding of the nature and inner workings of Eggs Iago with Greenblatt Sauce, also known as Huevos Iago con Salsa Verdeblatte. To prepare and enjoy Eggs Iago with Greenblatt Sauce one must first prepare the context in which the work is accomplished—or else the effect is all for naught.

Step 1: Turn off all the lights in the domicile. Turn the thermostat down all the way. Light a candle (a fairly large one), since you will be operating in the dark for a while.

Step 2: Prepare the Greenblatt Sauce. Go to a Spanish-speaking store or tienda, and buy 1 pound of tomatilloes, which should be green in a dusky sort of way. Then go to where the garlic is and get 4 cloves. Find 1 small onion willing to be part of all of this. Ask for some jalapeño chiles—just 2. Search for some really authentic-looking olive oil; buy a standard container of salt. Throw in some red chili peppers. Buy some sugar (because stealing packets from Starbucks will just get you in trouble). Ask for their best cilantro. Pay Maria at the cash register, smile, and wave Adiós.

Step 3: Go back to the domicile and notice that the candle is still burning and it's colder in the dark. Time to get to work. Take the husks off the tomatilloes, simmer for about

10 minutes, find the blender you got last year but never used. Propel the tomatilloes out of the simmering phase of their lives and into the blender, along with the garlic, chopped onions, cilantro, chiles, oil; purée away. Listen to the people upstairs tromping around, quietly curse them, and then notice that the top of the blender is about to come off. Secure the cap, then turn the blender off. [Whew, that was close.] Then pour the sauce into a saucepan and simmer over low heat, adding the salt, sugar, and pepper to taste. The Greenblatt Sauce should have the smoky taste of an accomplice to a crime. If this fails to materialize, fly to Albuquerque, New Mexico, and make your way to Old Town where there is a delicatessen on Mountain Road with a wide array of tomatillo salsas which are almost as good.

Step 4: Take 2 eggs, or 4 if you have a friend who is willing to try this. Since you are without the company of such a friend, just take the 2 eggs out of the refrigerator. Crack them open, and pour into a deep bowl; whisk in some milk or yogurt, or both—but just a little bit—keeping it all yellow. Pour a little of that authentic oil Maria suggested that you buy at the store into a frying pan and scramble the eggs just like Mom used to do. When they are nice and fluffy, take some ketchup packets that you swiped from Burger King and squeeze the contents into the cooking egg mixture This is the Iago factor of Eggs Iago. They should look like nice scars on the surface of the scrambled eggs—if not, then you have failed.

Step 5: Find some bread in the fridge and put 2 slices on a plate. Turn off the stove and ladle the scrambled Eggs Iago onto the bread; find the Greenblatt Sauce and spoon a sufficient amount onto the eggs and bread. Clear off some space on your cluttered table of unread used paperbacks, bills, and junk mail, place the sputtering candle in the center, and dive into your meal of Eggs Iago with Greenblatt Sauce. And as the effect of the smoky tomatillo-based Greenblatt Sauce and Eggs Iago take hold, contemplate those lines of Iago, in that misnamed play *Othello*, by the light of your candle:

> Do, with like timorous accent and dire yell
> As when, by night and negligence, the fire
> Is spied in populous cities.
>
> —*Iago*, 1.1. 75–77

Sincerely,
Steven C. Ballinger

The Warhol Kitchen Chard and Onion Omelet

Trouchia

Tim Sullivan

From Deborah Madison's Vegetarian Cooking for Everyone.

3 tablespoons olive oil
1 large red onion, thinly sliced
1 bunch chard, leaves only, chopped
salt and pepper to taste
3 garlic cloves, mashed
6–8 eggs, lightly beaten
2 tablespoons fresh parsley, chopped
2 tablespoons fresh basil, chopped
2 teaspoons fresh thyme, chopped
1 cup Gruyère (or Swiss) cheese, shredded
2 tablespoons Parmesan cheese

Heat 2 tablespoons oil in a 10-inch skillet, add onion and cook over low heat, stirring occasionally, until completely soft (about 15 minutes). Add the chard and continue cooking, stirring occasionally, until all the moisture has cooked off and the chard is tender, about 15 minutes. Season well with salt and pepper, then remove from the pan and set aside.

Mash the garlic with a few pinches of salt, and then stir into the eggs, along with the herbs. Combine the chard mixture with the eggs; stir in the Gruyère and half the Parmesan.

Preheat the broiler. Heat the remaining tablespoon of oil in the skillet and add the eggs. Give a stir and keep the heat at medium high for about a minute, then turn it to low. Cook until the eggs are set but still a little moist on the top, about 10–15 minutes. Sprinkle the remaining Parmesan on top and broil 4–6 inches from the heat, until browned. Serve in the pan, or slide onto a serving dish and cut into wedges.

Serves 4–6 people as a main dish.

Miscellaneous Quiche

Why Men Won't Ask for Directions Dale Cotton

Purchase 2 pre-made quiche crusts from Whole-in-Your-Wallet Foods.

Slide the gate across the kitchen doorway so the curious dogs cannot get in.

Look for a mixing bowl somewhere under the sink.

Look for the ingredients you thought you may have purchased a week ago.

Try to remember what you used last time it didn't work.

Add whatever ingredients you can find to the bowl.

Figure out how to create enough liquid to fill the 2 crusts.

When you cannot fill the 2 crusts, add vodka to fill the gap.

Try to remember what temperature to use for the oven.

Try to remember if you need to pre-heat or just put it in there.

Watch TV for at least 45 minutes before you obsess over checking the oven.

Once you've forgotten to check the oven, get there fast and stick a fork in it.

If it's sticky, you're good.

Try to eat it.

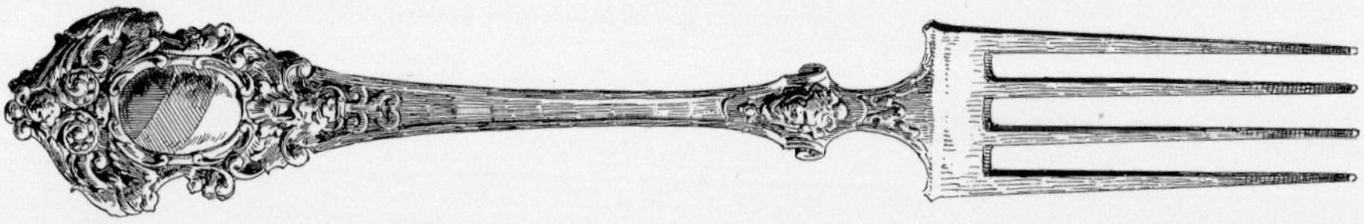

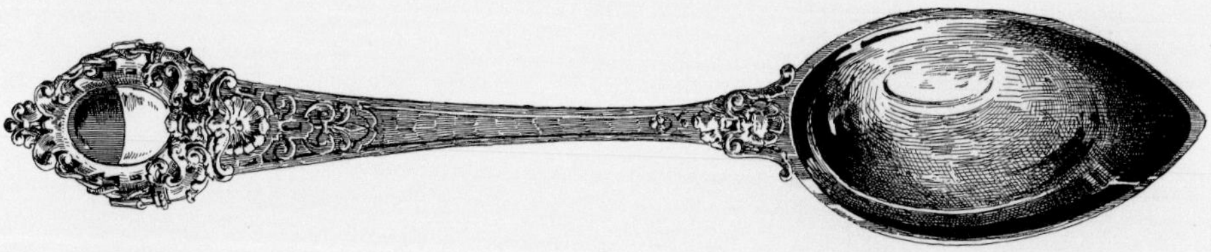

Gottschalk Grillades

Sarah Van Kirk

This is a classic Creole brunch dish that's served all over the place in New Orleans. The only thing Gottschalk liked more than playing the piano was this dish.

Ideally, grillades should be served over grits. I don't really recommend it over cheesy grits. If you'd like to eat it for dinner, or you simply don't like grits, rice makes a reasonable substitute.

4 cloves garlic, roasted, divided use
2 tablespoons salt
½ teaspoon red pepper
1 teaspoon thyme
1 teaspoon black pepper
1 teaspoon paprika
a 2½-pound round steak, ½-inch thick
olive oil
¾ cup green bell pepper, diced
¾ cup celery, diced
2¼ cup onions, diced
2 teaspoons browned flour
2 teaspoons cold water
1 12-ounce can of tomato paste
3 cups boiling water

Preheat oven to 275 degrees (F).

To brown flour toast it in a dry pan on the stove. Keep an eye on it, for it will burn easily. (It's easier to make this in large quantities; it will last forever, so toast about a ½ cup at a time and keep the excess in a jar.)

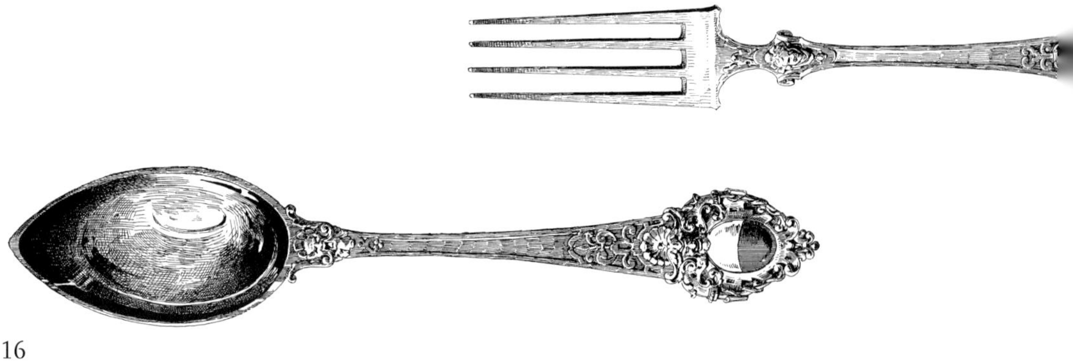

Make a paste of a 3 cloves of garlic, plus salt, red pepper, thyme, black pepper, and paprika. Taste to see if more salt is needed and adjust as necessary. (This paste will freeze forever.)

Pound the meat with a meat hammer until it is twice its original size. Rub paste into both sides of meat. Do not be overgenerous, aim for a light coating. Cut meat into pieces the size of a deck of playing cards. In a large Dutch oven, brown the pieces in olive oil. Mince the last clove of garlic. Add it and veggies to oil. Cook over medium heat, stirring frequently, until veggies are just soft.

While the veggies cook: in a small bowl, mix 2 teaspoons of browned flour and 2 teaspoons of cold water with a fork to make a slurry. Add 1 can of tomato paste and 3 cups boiling water to veggies and meat. Stir. Mix in slurry.

Put lid on pot and put it in the oven; bake till meat is tender (roughly 45 minutes). The sauce should still be thin. Remove from oven, adjust seasonings to taste, and serve.

What to do with leftovers?

It freezes nicely, so you can pop it in and enjoy it much later. Also, if you've made Bob's grits and have some left over, follow his directions for cutting leftover grits into squares for pan frying. Your grillades will be equally yummy the next day over fried grits.

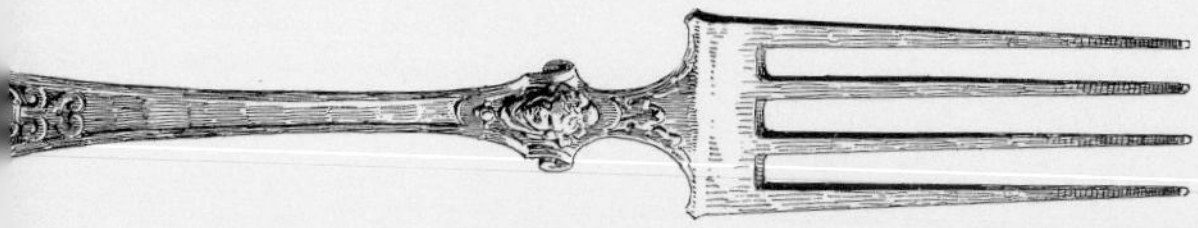

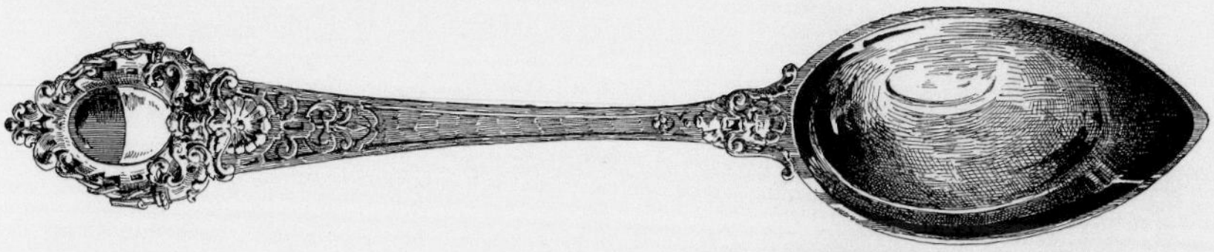

Lost in the Syrup French Toast Casserole

Debbie Greco

This is a great dish for a holiday brunch or for treating yourself on the weekend. It is prepared the night before and baked in the morning. It is even scrumptious as a leftover.

TOAST
1–2 loaves good quality bakery or
home-baked white bread (unsliced)

EGG MIXTURE
5 eggs
1½ cup milk
1 teaspoon vanilla extract
¼ teaspoon salt

SYRUP
2 tablespoons corn syrup
½ cup butter
1 cup brown sugar, packed

Begin preparation the night before. Simmer corn syrup, butter, and brown sugar until syrupy. Pour into a deep 9 x 13–inch baking dish. Slice the bread into thick slices, remove crusts, and place on the syrup in two even, tightly packed layers. Beat together eggs, milk, vanilla extract, and salt; pour evenly over the bread. Cover and refrigerate overnight.

In the morning, preheat oven to 350 degrees (F). Leave casserole at room temperature while oven preheats. Bake uncovered, for 45 minutes. Top should be browned. Cut into squares and serve immediately.

You can serve with butter and maple syrup, but they're not necessary.

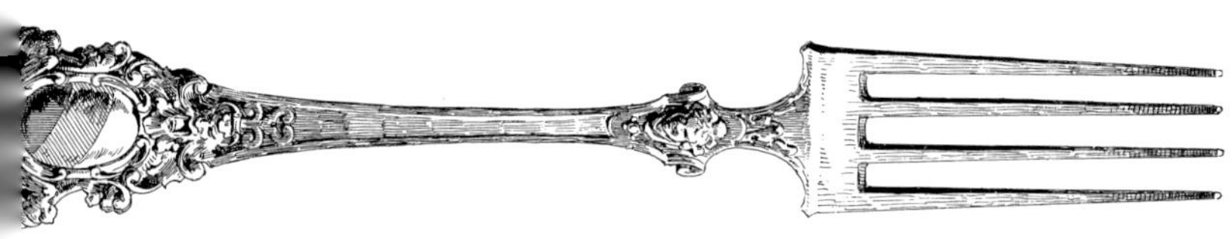

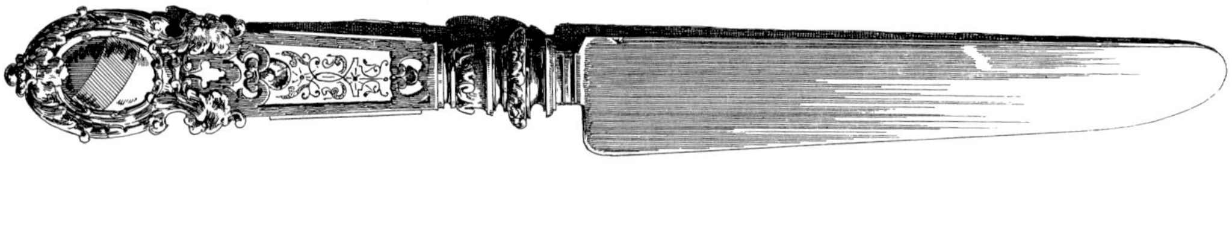

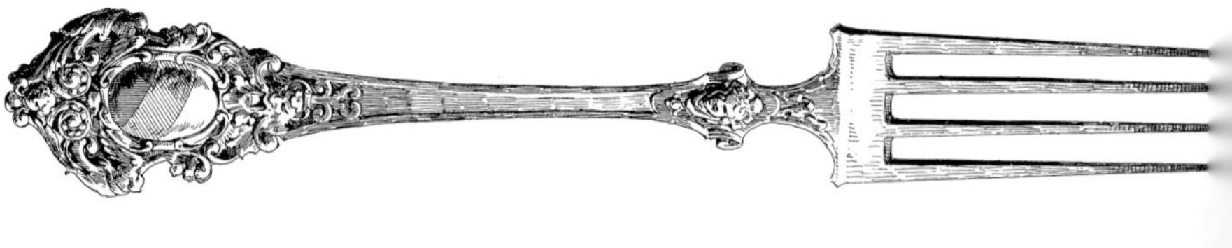

Why the French Don't Hate Baked Blueberry French Toast

Michele LaForge

1 loaf heavy delicioso artisanal bread, multigrain, or
other chunky bread, sliced
6 eggs
½ cup milk
¼ teaspoon baking powder
1½ teaspoons vanilla extract
3 (or more) cups blueberries and/or raspberries
(mixed berries and frozen berries work fine)
½ cup sugar
1 teaspoon cinnamon
1 teaspoon cornstarch
1 tablespoon butter, melted
powdered sugar

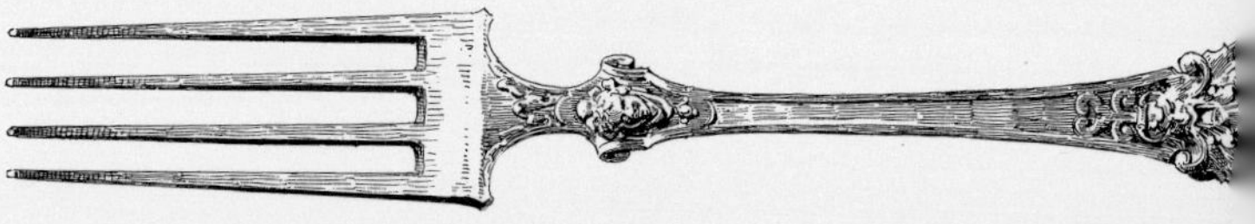

Preheat oven at 350 degrees (F).

Grease a jelly roll pan or large cookie sheet with sides.

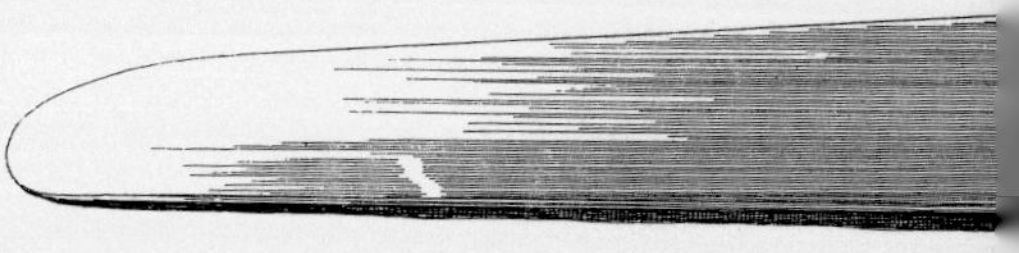

Mix together berries, sugar, cinnamon, and cornstarch; sprinkle over the bottom of the prepared pan or sheet. In a medium-large bowl, whip together eggs, milk, baking powder, and vanilla extract.

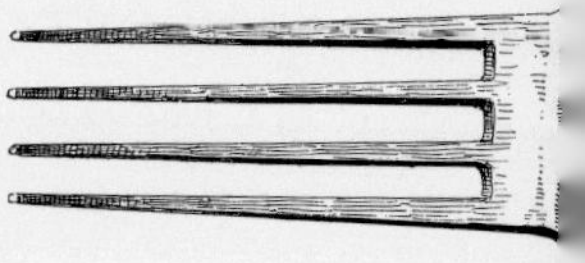

Slowly soak bread slices, one at a time, in egg mixture, bringing slices back for more soaking to make sure you get them as eggy as you like—but not so much that they are dripping or runny. Tightly wedge bread slices on top of the berries in a single layer on the jelly roll pan or cookie sheet. Brush the top of the bread with a little melted butter.

Bake uncovered in the center of the oven for 20–25 minutes, or until golden brown.

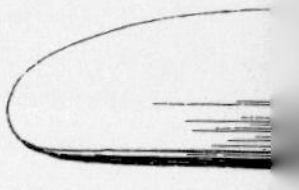

To serve, place the toast berry-side down and scoop up any extra berry mixture onto the plate. Sprinkle with powdered sugar. Serve as is, or with maple syrup. (I do the latter, of course. And rarely do I sprinkle with powdered sugar…the bread just doesn't make it that far before getting gobbled up.)

For those of you with kids, my kids love this cut into French toast strips. Mmmmm.

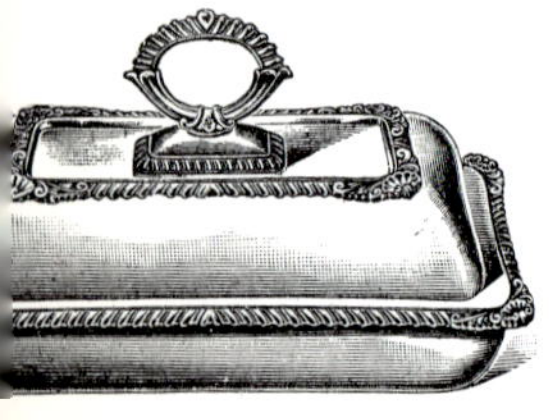

Main (Dis)Courses I

Beastly Ethics

Dishes with Meat

The Barrington Atlas of the Greek and Roman Chicken

Margret Aldrich

Your dinner guests won't need a map to find their way to the table when they smell this delicious dish cooking! For best results, use Bell & Evans chicken, Muir Glen tomatoes, and wine that is good enough to drink with the meal. If you'd like to serve more people, you can increase the number of chicken pieces up to 6, as long as they fit in your pan. Feel free to use skinless chicken thighs (with bones) if you prefer dark meat, or use a combination of breasts and thighs. This is based on a recipe from Giada De Laurentiis's program Everyday Italian.

4 skinless chicken breast halves, with bones
salt and freshly ground pepper
¼ cup olive oil
3 ounces prosciutto, chopped
2 bell peppers (preferably 1 yellow and 1 red), sliced lengthwise
2 cloves garlic, chopped
½ cup white wine
1 15-ounce can diced tomatoes
1 tablespoon fresh thyme
⅓ teaspoon dried oregano
½ cup chicken stock
¼ cup fresh flat-leaf parsley, chopped
2 tablespoons capers (or substitute ¼ cup pitted kalamata olives, roughly chopped)

Season the chicken on both sides with salt and pepper. Heat the olive oil over medium heat in a large skillet (note that you will need a lid for it later). Add the chicken to the pan and brown it on both sides. Remove the chicken to a plate; set aside.

Add the prosciutto and peppers to the original pan and cook over medium heat for 5 minutes. Add the garlic and cook for 1 minute. Add the wine, tomatoes, thyme, and oregano, and use a wooden spoon to scrape the browned bits off the bottom of the pan.

Return the chicken and any accumulated juices to the pan, add the stock, and bring it to a boil. Cover with the lid, reduce the heat, and simmer for 20–30 minutes, until the chicken is done. Taste and add a bit more salt and pepper, if desired. Stir in the parsley and capers (or olives) and serve.

Serves 4.

Cyber Goddess "Great White North" Chilly

Revenge of the Once-Domestic Canadian Ann Ambrose

1 pound ground chicken or veggie ground round
1 medium-sized onion, chopped
1 can stewed tomatoes
1 can tomato sauce
1 can pork and beans
1–2 tablespoons chili powder

Sauté chicken and onion in large frying pan. Add tomatoes, sauce, beans, and chili powder; stir. Simmer for 45 minutes to 1 hour; alternatively, throw ingredients into slow cooker and cook on low for the day (or at least 6 hours).

Serves 4.

Note for Canadians: Many apologies for the nonmetric measurements. Substitute 10 kilograms of whale blubber for ground chicken. Add an additional kilogram of chili powder and serve with a side of rubaboo.

Serves 12, plus 8 sled dogs.

Is Pasta a Planet?

Unexpected Orbits with Peppered Chicken

Brigitte Pelner

8 chicken tenders or 2 chicken cutlets
½ cup or more mushrooms
black pepper, cracked
1 teaspoon dried tarragon
½ cup or more Chablis or other white wine
2–3 tablespoons butter (divided use)
enough mutligrain rotini for two people

Start the water boiling for the pasta a couple of minutes before dressing the chicken, so the pasta will be done at around the same time. (It takes only about 10–15 minutes to prepare the rest of the meal.)

Sprinkle and press cracked pepper onto the chicken pieces. Add a bit of salt too, if desired. Melt 1–2 tablespoons butter in a skillet over medium heat, and then sauté the chicken—about 3 minutes for each side, or until it looks done. (Note: It's best *not* to use a nonstick pan when you sauté the chicken because you want to have browned cooked-on bits left in the pan for scraping later, for flavor.) Remove the chicken from the pan and keep it on a plate until later.

Slice the mushrooms or cut them into chunks. Melt another 1–2 tablespoons butter in the original skillet, and then add tarragon blending it into the butter. Add the mushrooms to the pan and sauté, stirring a bit to cook them evenly. When the mushrooms are nicely browned, add the wine to the pan. Make sure to scrape the skillet thoroughly to combine all the remaining cooked-on bits with the wine.

Return the chicken to the skillet; let it simmer in the wine for a minute or so. While the chicken is simmering, check to be sure the pasta is done; when ready, drain in a colander and then return pasta to the pot it was cooked in. Remove the chicken and mushrooms and arrange them on dinner plates or serving platter.

Pour the remaining cooked wine mixture into the pasta pot and toss. Then add the pasta to the dinner plates.

Serves 2.
For a vegetable, I reccomend asparagus with this meal.

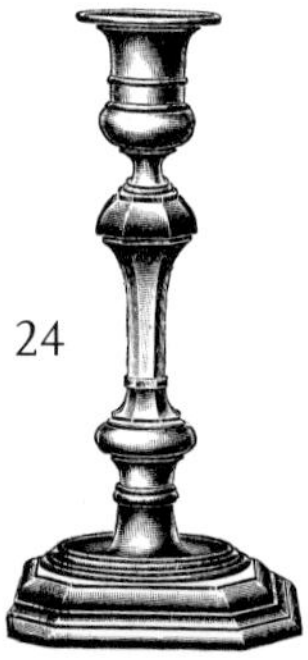

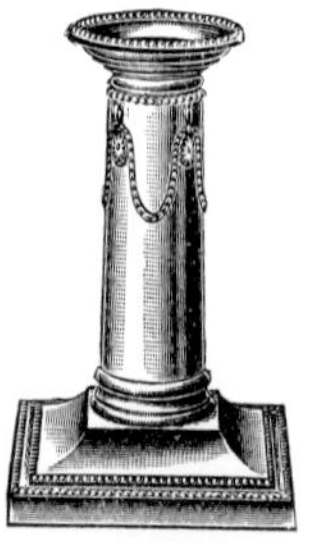

Matthew Roller Longevity Noodles

Jeremy Wang-Iverson

This recipe is named in honor of Dining Posture in Ancient Rome *scribe Matthew Roller. It comes from the Shang Dynasty (~1600 BC). You serve it on birthdays and then you live a long time.*

There's no better way to analyze your friends' and loved ones' dining postures than by serving them up some longevity noodles and then surreptitiously observing them.

He puts her arm around her—what can it mean?

Now he crosses his right leg over her left leg!

1 pound lo mein or egg noodles
2–3 scallions, including green tops,
  cut into ¼" pieces
8–11 slices fresh ginger
8–11 cloves crushed garlic
2 tablespoons vegetable oil
sesame oil
½ cup chicken broth
½ pound shrimp, shelled and deveined
½ pound pork, sliced in ⅛ x 1" pieces
1 pound fresh spinach
bamboo shoots, thinly sliced
3–4 large Chinese mushrooms, softened (soak in
  water) and sliced in strips
½ head any variety Chinese cabbage, chopped

Cook noodles according to package directions and drain; add sesame oil to keep noodles from sticking. Heat vegetable oil in a saucepan; add 3–4 slices ginger and 3 crushed garlic cloves; stir for 2 minutes over medium heat; add shrimp and sauté until pink; season with salt and pepper; set aside. In another saucepan, heat 1–2 tablespoons vegetable oil; add scallions and sauté. Add 3–4 slices ginger, and 3–4 crushed garlic cloves. Add bamboo shoots and Chinese mushrooms; sauté for 2 minutes. Add Chinese cabbage; mix for 3–4 minutes. Add spinach; mix for 3–4 more minutes. Season to taste with salt and pepper; add chicken broth and continue cooking. Add shrimp and pork mixture to vegetable mixture; mix well. Combine with noodles.

Just before serving, you might brown the dish under a broiler.

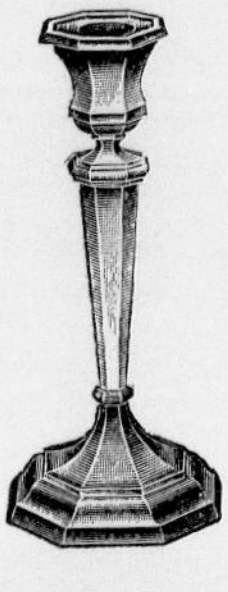

Revisiting Rosemary Chicken with Embedded Baby Red Bliss Potatoes

Lorraine Doneker

2–4 pounds chicken parts (washed)
2–3 cloves garlic
¼ cup olive oil
¼ cup bread crumbs
¼ cup shredded fresh Parmesan cheese
4 tablespoons chopped fresh rosemary, divided use
¼ teaspoon black pepper
1 small bag baby red bliss potatoes
(about 10–15), halved

Preheat oven to 425 degrees (F).

Mix olive oil and crushed garlic with 2 tablespoons fresh rosemary. In another small bowl mix the bread crumbs, pepper, cheese, and 2 tablespoons rosemary.

Spread the chicken pieces on a flat baking dish; if skin is on, place skin side up. Wash and halve the small potatoes (do not peel), and tuck them around the chicken pieces, with skin sides down. Sprinkle the breadcrumb mixture over the chicken pieces and the potatoes; then sprinkle the olive oil mixture on the pieces. Place in oven for 15 minutes. After 15 minutes, lower the temperature to 350, and continue baking for 40–50 minutes.

Can be served with roasted asparagus. Keep asparagus long and drizzle with oil and garlic; lay side by side and roast approximately 30 minutes, or to desired firmness.

Salad can be prepared ahead of time, and can be served with this dish, along with your favorite bread or rolls.

For a quick and tasty dessert, a Cold Stone Creamery cake is the ticket!

The Myth of the Rational Midwesterner

Quayle-Free Ham and Potato[e] Casserole Mark Bellis

For people who don't like to cook, it doesn't get much easier than this—even if you hail from Indiana (not unlike myself and a certain former vice-president of the United States). The best part is that this is the kind of dish that's even better when it's reheated on the second day. Good with asparagus.

1 pound cubed cooked ham
4 medium russet potatoes, skinned and sliced
1 small white onion, sliced
2 cups grated cheddar cheese
¾ cup whole milk
1 tablespoon all-purpose flour
salt and ground pepper

Preheat oven to 350 degrees (F).

Coat an 8 x 10-inch baking dish with cooking spray, and layer half of the potatoes. Sprinkle potatoes with flour, salt, and pepper. Layer all of the cubed ham, half the onion slices, and half the grated cheese. Add the rest of the potatoes and season again with salt and pepper. Add remaining onions and top with remaining cheese. Pour milk over all, cover with aluminum foil, and bake until bubbly (about 1 hour). Remove foil and let stand for a few minutes before serving.

Makes about 6 servings.

Recasting Bourgeois Halupkies

Stuffed Cabbage Rolls

Bill McDonald

This recipe comes from www.coalregion.com ("Straight outta da Coal Region kitchen"); the dish is also know as "galumpkies," or (in American) "blind pigeons."

1 head cabbage (about 3 pounds)
1 pound ground pork
1 pound ground beef
1 tablespoon salt
½ teaspoon pepper
1 can stewed tomatoes (or substitute Campbell's
    tomato soup, undiluted)
¾ cup uncooked rice
1 onion, chopped
1 tablespoon shortening

Cut into cabbage deeply around the core to loosen and remove the leaves. Boil the cabbage leaves about 5 minutes; set aside to drain.

In a skillet, add ground meats, onions, shortening, salt, and pepper; fry slowly for about 15 minutes.

Wash rice, drain, and add to meat; mix well.

Place 1 tablespoon of the meat mixture in the center of each cabbage leaf and roll it up. Place rolled leaves side by side in pot. Pour tomatoes (or soup) over top and add enough water to cover. Add another tablespoon each salt and pepper.

Cook 1½ hours.

Cooking-Aided Verification of Marinating Processes

The Pork Tenderloin Approach

Lucy Day Hobor

My husband and I often marinate and cook two tenderloins at once because the leftover pork is good cold. I like to eat it with bread, especially if we've made bread in the breadmaker. This recipe is adapted from one we found at Sunset Foods in Highland Park, Illinois.

10–14 ounces pork tenderloin
½ cup olive oil
¾ cup soy sauce
2 cloves crushed garlic
¼ cup Worcestershire sauce
2 teaspoons dry mustard
dash of dried oregano
dash of dried basil
dash of salt and pepper

Mix all ingredients (except tenderloin) in a bowl, for marinade.

Slice the tenderloin into thirds to increase the surface area and place the pieces in a flat-bottomed container. Pour marinade from bowl over pork, seal, and refrigerate for 1 hour.

After marinating, preheat oven to 350 degrees (F).

Transfer pork to a roasting pan and bake for 35–40 minutes. Use the marinade to baste the tenderloin halfway through the cooking process. Remove from oven and slice diagonally to serve.

Serves 2–3.

Low-Paperwork Pastitsio with Benefits

Persa Ducko

Pastitsio
½ cup butter
2 pounds ground beef
1 onion, chopped
1 cup dry white wine
2 tomatoes, peeled and sliced
3-tablespoons parsley, chopped
1½ teaspoons salt
1 teaspoon cinnamon
½ teaspoon pepper
1 cup grated Parmesan cheese
3 tablespoons bread crumbs
1 pound ziti macaroni
4 egg whites (reserve the yolks for sauce)
½ cup butter

Sauce
6 tablespoons butter
6 tablespoons flour
2 cups boiling chicken broth
2 cups warm milk
4 egg yolks, beaten

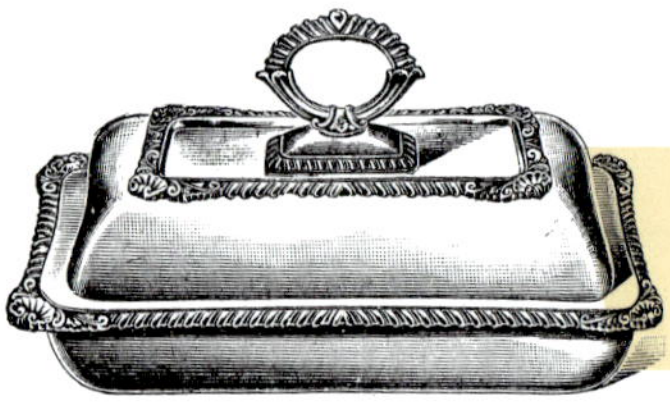

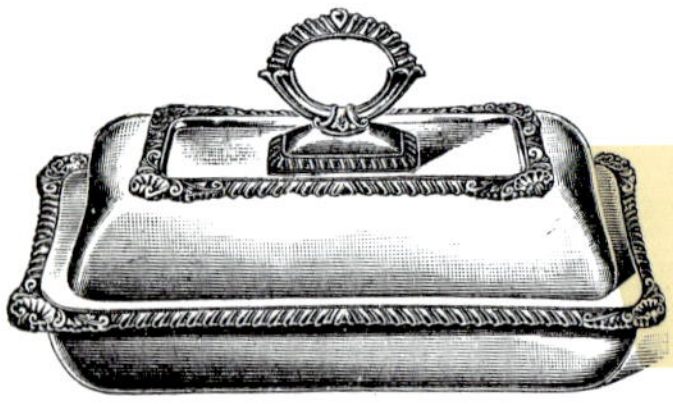

Pastitsio

Preheat oven to 350 degrees (F).

Sauté onion in ½ cup butter; set aside. Brown the beef, and mix in onion. When meat sizzles, add wine. Stir and add tomatoes, parsley, salt, cinnamon, and pepper. Simmer, covered, for about ½ hour. Add 2 tablespoons cheese and the bread crumbs. Stir and let stand. Cook ziti macaroni in boiling water, and then drain. Stir the egg whites into the macaroni along with the ½ cup butter and all but 2 tablespoons of the remaining cheese. Toss to combine.

Make the sauce (see below).

Place half the macaroni in a deep 9 x 13-inch baking pan and cover with the meat mixture. Layer the rest of the macaroni onto the meat mixture and cover with the sauce. With a spatula, push some of the sauce around the inside of the pan. Sprinkle the rest of the cheese over the top.

Bake in oven until the top is golden and the sauce set—about 45 minutes. Remove from oven and let stand 10–15 minutes before serving.

Sauce

In a saucepan, melt butter over low heat. Using a wire whisk, stir in flour and blend well. Remove from heat. Gradually stir in broth and milk; then stir vigorously. Return to heat and cook, stirring constantly, until sauce is thick and smooth.

Stir a little of the hot sauce into the egg yolks. Stir yolk mixture into sauce and cook over very low heat for 2 minutes, stirring constantly.

Serves 12 as a main course.

Shani's Choulent in Translation

Shani Nabet

"Choulent" comes from the French and means "slow-cooked." This is a modern adaptation of an age-old recipe from the cold shtetls of Russia and Poland. Better than soup, this slow-cooked stew will warm you on the coldest of winter nights.

- 2 cups barley (or 1 cup barely and 1 cup mixed beans)
- 2 large potatoes
- 2 large sweet potatoes
- 2 large carrots
- 1 large onion
- 1 can chickpeas (optional)
- 2 pounds stewing meat such as brisket, ribs, or lamb chops
- a few soup bones for flavor
- ½ teaspoon salt
- ½ teaspoon pepper
- 1 teaspoon paprika
- ½ teaspoon garlic powder
- ½–¾ cup ketchup or barbecue sauce
- ½ cup honey
- water

Cover the inside of a 4- to 6-quart slow cooker with cooking spray for easy cleaning. Place barley (and beans) at bottom of pot. Coarsely chop vegetables into 1-inch chunks, and add full can of chickpeas. Combine and place on top of barley. Place meat on top of vegetables. Add salt, pepper, paprika, garlic powder, ketchup or barbecue sauce, and honey. Add just enough water to cover all ingredients.

Prepare ingredients in the morning; cook all day on high heat to be ready for dinner when you get home from work. Or prepare the night before and cook on low heat overnight and all the following day for dinner the next night.

Do not worry about overcooking—the longer a choulent stays in the pot, the more savory it becomes. Freeze leftovers immediately for up to 2 months, or reheat in microwave for a delicious lunch.

Scribner's Scrumptious Stuffed-Shell Tacos

Gary Beck

Chef's notes: Any ingredient/instruction marked "optional" might as well read "omit"; any step that can be skipped is one step closer to eating. For those on a vegetarian or a low- or no-fat diet, simply disregard entire recipe and have a salad.

1¼ pound ground beef
3 ounces cream cheese with chives, cubed
 and softened
1 teaspoon salt
1 teaspoon chili powder
18 jumbo pasta shells, cooked, rinsed, and drained
2 tablespoons butter, melted
1 cup prepared taco sauce
1 cup shredded cheddar cheese
1 cup shredded Monterey Jack cheese
1½ cups crushed tortilla chips
1 cup sour cream
3 green onions, chopped
leaf lettuce (optional)
small ripe olives, pitted (optional)
cherry tomatoes (optional)

Preheat oven to 350 degrees (F).

Cook ground beef in large skillet over medium-high heat until brown, stirring to separate meat; drain fatty grease waste. (*Chef's note*: Be sure to drain fatty grease waste into a safe container. It is not recommended that fat be drained down the sink or into your wife's coffee. Trust me.) Reduce heat to medium low. Add cream cheese, salt, and chili powder; simmer 5 minutes.

Toss shells with butter; fill with beef mixture. Arrange shells in a buttered 13 x 9-inch pan, and cover with foil. Bake in oven for 15 minutes. Uncover, top with cheddar cheese, Monterey Jack cheese, and chips. Recover, and bake for 15 minutes more, or until bubbly.

Remove. Top with sour cream and onions. Garnish with the optionals: lettuce, olives, and tomatoes.

Yield—if you've been paying attention—18 stuffed shells.

Topics in Harmonic Shrimp, Chicken, and Andouille Sausage Gumbo

Eileen Reilly

Gumbo base

½ cup vegetable oil
½ cup all-purpose flour
3 large onions, chopped (to make about 6 cups)
3 red bell peppers, seeded and chopped (about 3 cups)
4 celery stalks, chopped (about 1-½ cups)
8 garlic cloves, chopped
½ teaspoon cayenne pepper
½ cup dry white wine
¼ cup chopped fresh thyme
3 bay leaves
1 28-ounce can diced tomatoes, with juice
2 8-ounce bottles clam juice
2 cups low-salt chicken broth

Meat

2 pounds nice, smoky, firm andouille sausage, cut crosswise into ½-inch slices
1½ pounds skinless boneless chicken breasts, cut into 1-inch cubes
16-ounce package sliced frozen okra (fresh okra is better, obviously)
2 pounds peeled, deveined medium shrimp (if you use frozen shrimp, thaw ahead of time)
steamed rice

Gumbo base

Heat oil in a heavy 7½–quart pot over medium-high heat until very hot and almost smoking. Add flour and stir constantly until mixture is a dark reddish brown—about 5 minutes. Add chopped onions, chopped bell peppers, and chopped celery; cook until onions are soft and brown, stirring frequently—about 20 minutes. Add garlic and cayenne; stir 2 minutes. Add wine, thyme, and bay leaves; bring to boil, stirring occasionally. Add tomatoes with juice, clam juice, broth, sausage, and chicken; simmer until chicken is cooked through—about 15 minutes. Add okra and simmer until tender—about 10 minutes. Cool slightly. Chill uncovered until cold, then cover and keep chilled.

Bring base to simmer before continuing.

Meat

Add shrimp to gumbo pot and cook until shrimp are just opaque in center, stirring often—about 5 minutes. Season gumbo to taste with salt and pepper. Garnish with minced parsley and serve with steamed rice alongside.

Gumbo base can be made 2 days ahead, and it's actually better if you do—it gives the flavors a chance to come through.

T. rex and the Crater of Barbecue

Formerly Known as "Jurassic Pork"

Eric Rohmann

This is a traditional pulled pork barbecue recipe requiring preparation the night before and a full day of slow cooking. I make it in a Weber kettle, but I presume any closed cover outdoor charcoal or gas grill will work.

Special ingredients

I use a special rub and barbecue sauces from Dinosaur Barbecue, available online at www.dinosaurbarbeque.com. I use the "Cajun Foreplay" rub for the meat and "Sensuous Slathering Sauce" souped up with their "Wango Tango" sauce. Of course you can use other spice rubs and sauces, but then you'd have to call it something other than Jurassic Pork.

For the pork

The best cut to use is Boston butt; however, a fresh ham or a picnic ham can be substituted. If using a picnic ham, you'll have to cut off the remaining skin—being sure to leave as much of the fat you can. Tony supermarkets don't stock Boston butt (too low-class), but you can find it if you look...and it's best because it is fatty throughout, so it remains moist and tender after smoking and baking.

Ingredients

68 pounds Boston butt or picnic ham (I ask for the biggest one they have)
⅓ to ½ cup spice rub
½ bottle dark beer
1 cup barbecue sauce, plus more, as desired, to add when making sandwiches
hamburger buns
cole slaw (optional)

Stuff we assume you have on hand

hickory chips for smoking
charcoal
disposable aluminum roasting pan, just slightly larger than the roast
heavy-duty aluminum foil
plastic wrap
supermarket paper grocery bag

The night before

Wash the pork in cold water and pat dry. Sprinkle spice rub all over the pork and massage in. Wrap tightly in plastic wrap and store (I put it in the roasting pan) in refrigerator overnight.

Next morning

Soak the wood chips in cold water about an hour before you start grilling.

Set up grill for indirect cooking: divide charcoal into two piles, one on each side of the grill. (Weber has charcoal baskets for this purpose, plus a grill with flip-up sides, so you can refill the baskets as necessary during the cooking.) You want a slow fire (average temperature in the grill should be 275 degrees (F), and you'll need to add 3 or 4 charcoal briquettes and more wood chips to each side every half-hour or so while you're smoking and cooking the roast.

Take the pork out of the refrigerator, remove the plastic wrap (take a whiff—hmm, hmm!) and put the pork into the roasting pan, fattier side up.

Place the roasting pan in the center of the grill; put a few soaked wood chips directly onto the charcoal, one on each side; make sure all the vents in the grill are open, and put on the lid. Wait.

Smoke/cook the roast for about 3 hours, adding charcoal and wood chips as necessary. Check frequently (at least once every half-hour) to make sure the fire is going and the wood chips are smoking—but don't stoke the fire too high. You don't want it to be cooking at higher than about 300 degrees. (In fact the more I make this, the lower the temperature I use. Don't worry about blackening to the top of the roast, although that might be an indication that you've got too much heat.)

About 2 hours into the smoking/roasting, when the juices are flowing, add about a half-bottle of some good-tasting beer. Just slosh it in and watch it foam! (You can drink the rest yourself!)

After about 3 hours, take the roasting pan off the grill, cover tightly with heavy-duty aluminum foil, and put the pan into a preheated oven (325 degrees F). Bone should be showing, top should be blackened, meat should be getting tender. (And by now it really smells good!)

Bake for an additional 2 hours, or until the meat is falling off the bone.

Remove from oven and slide the covered roasting pan into a plastic grocery bag; let sit for 1 hour or so, to allow the juices to be somewhat reabsorbed (which makes the meat juicy and tender). After 1 hour or so, the meat should be cool enough to handle.

Open the bag, remove the meat, and place it on a cutting board; separate into workable chunks—it should pull apart into muscle segments.

In a small saucepan, warm the barbecue sauce (about one-half bottle). Add some Wango Tango sauce, or Tabasco, or whatever you like. Or just leave plain.

Then "pull" the meat apart into strands. (I used to use my fingers for this, but I've discovered that it's easier— and quicker!— to use two forks: take a chunk of meat and tear it apart into long strands with the forks.) Retain as much of the fat as you wish while pulling (I usually remove some fat, since I don't want the meat to be greasy).

Layer the strands of meat into a large ovenproof bowl and add some barbecue sauce to each layer as you work. (Don't use too much sauce—there will be more on the table to add as needed, and the pork itself already has plenty of flavor from the rub and the smoking. I understand that you can also chop the pork—that is, hack it up with a kitchen knife—rather than pulling it; I've not tried this.)

The top of the roast will be blackened and crispy; slice it off and chop it fine, sprinkling among the layers of meat and adding some to the sauce you've got heating on the stove. You don't want that Cajun Foreplay rub to go to waste, right?

Toss the meat from time to time to mix in the sauce. Since the meat is hot and can take a while to pull, I usually reheat it in the microwave before serving— giving it another toss and a couple of buzzes.

Serve on hamburger buns or white bread. This is not fancy food and it would be terrible on multigrain breads. This is shit-kicker food and it should be served that way. Some like to put coleslaw in the sandwich with the pork. Help yourself! Put more sauce on the table for people who want more.

We serve it with potato salad and bean casserole, but you can serve it with anything and it will still be delicious.

Yield: quite a lot! We serve it to a dozen and there's leftovers.

Main (Dis)courses II

The Afterlives of Vegetables

Vegetarian Dishes

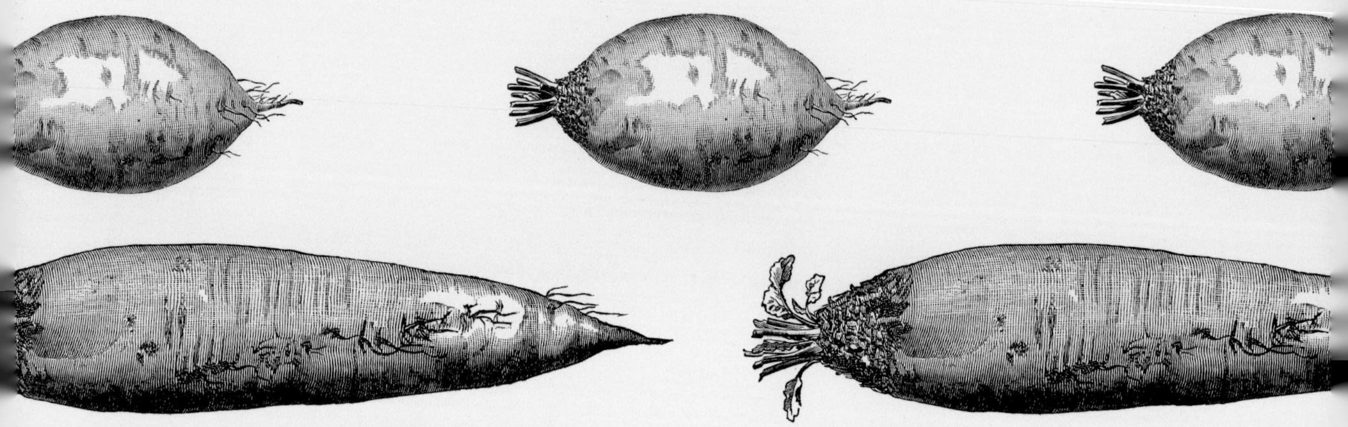

Kasha's Metamorphosis

Neil Litt

Food and memory are inextricably linked. But what happens when the flavor of a beloved dish from childhood is altered slightly, just enough to make everything feel off? In my experience, the results can range from mild disappointment to enervating distemper. The other night, to go along with some leftover brisket from my family Hanukkah party, I made kasha varnishkes. I tweaked my mom's recipe a bit. It was a terrible, horrible mistake.

—confession of Debbie ——, of Williamsburg in Brooklyn, NY, on her food blog, at http://wordstoeatby.blogspot.com/2004/12/madeleines-shmadeleines-kasha.html.

Yet sometimes it can be an error of equal magnitude to go home again and eat exactly what we remember. My return to the Eastern European restaurants of the Lower East Side, in search of the kasha varnishkes of my youth, was no less horrible than Debbie's "tweak." Kasha is more texture than taste and my hunger for the texture has not abated, but the thick and salty beef gravy that I loved as a boy no longer charms. (And a good thing! Like the schmaltz my uncle used to smear on Wonder Bread, it's a royal invitation to congestive heart failure!)

The following recipe is a better reflection of the Lower East Side as it is now than as it was then. Today, the last Jewish remnants are the shops that sell Sefer Torot, surrounded by the expanding Chinese presence overflowing the old boundaries of Chinatown. In that spirit, I mix my kasha with stir-fried vegetables.

I use coarse-grained kasha, and while this recipe works with all manner of kasha, my hunger (as I already mentioned) is for the texture.

1 cup kasha (buckwheat groats)
1 egg, beaten
2 cups vegetable broth (hot)
1 large onion cut in strips
½ pound mushrooms
1 red pepper
1 stalk broccoli cut into small pieces
olive oil
soy sauce

Mix 1 cup of kasha with the beaten egg and then toss the mixture into a medium-sized frying pan over moderate heat, stirring constantly until the grains separate and begin to dry. Pour the 2 cups of vegetable broth over the mixture, reduce the heat to a low setting, and cover the pan. Remove from the heat and set aside once all the liquid is absorbed (10–15 minutes).

While the kasha is simmering, stir-fry the onions in a large, oiled frying pan over high flame until they begin to soften, then add mushrooms and red pepper. Mix thoroughly, generously add soy sauce, and keep mixing. Throw in the broccoli and keep mixing. You may want to steam the broccoli first but you may not. Life is full of choices. It's ready when you think it's ready; after which you should remove from heat, pour the kasha in, and mix thoroughly.

Subprime Squash Casserole Solution with Completed Task List

Elizabeth Byrd

6 slices cooked bacon, crumbled
8 yellow squash
1 sliced onion
6–8 ounces cheddar cheese, shredded
1 egg
10–12 Saltines

Preheat oven to 325 degrees (F).
Cook squash and onion on low, no water. Season with salt and pepper.
Fry bacon and crumble. Mix all together, except cheese.
Place in dish, top with shredded cheese. Bake for about 30 minutes.

Why a Pizza Is Like a Painting

Leslie Flis

3–4 heads garlic
3–4 tablespoons olive oil
2 large sweet onions
2–3 tablespoons balsamic vinegar
4–6 Portabella mushroom caps, sliced
3–4 cups diced butternut squash
½–1 teaspoon dried thyme, or fresh thyme
½ cup shelled pistachio nuts
½–1 cup cheese (optional) of your choice (goat, brie, mozzarella, or freshly grated Parmesan work well, but it's also good without cheese)
pizza crust of your choice (homemade, Bobolis, flatbreads, or some pocket-less pitas work well)
3–4 anchovy fillets (optional)
freshly ground course pepper

Preheat oven to 375–400 degrees (F).

Cut the tops off garlic heads, place on foil, drizzle with about a tablespoon olive oil, wrap in foil, and bake for at least 45 minutes. Cool long enough to handle, then squish out the garlic, and mash it with another tablespoon olive oil. (If you like anchovies, take 3–4 anchovy fillets and mash them along with the garlic.)

Slice onions into ¼-inch slices and sauté with olive oil till brown and sticky; deglaze the pan with balsamic vinegar and remove onions from pan.

Sauté the mushroom slices in same pan with a little more olive oil, till nice and brown; remove from pan.

Sauté the diced butternut squash with a little more olive oil and thyme till barely tender, not mushy.

Place your pizza crust on a pizza stone or pan; spread with garlic and artfully arrange remaining toppings; add cheese (optional) and sprinkle with the pistachios. Bake for about 25 mintues, but check after 20 minutes.

Add a tossed salad and pour a glass of Shiraz and you are set!
Enjoy!

Princeton Encyclopedia of Wild Mushroom Pasta Gratin

Anne Savarese

1 ounce dried porcini
3 tablespoons unsalted butter (divided use)
1 tablespoon all-purpose flour
1½ cups vegetable or chicken broth
1 cup heavy cream
salt and pepper
nutmeg
½ pound assorted fresh mushrooms
2 cloves garlic, minced or put through a press
2 tablespoons chopped parsley
1 pound fettuccine (or any other wide, flat pasta)
Parmesan cheese for grating

Preheat the oven to 425 degrees (F).

Put dried porcini in a bowl and cover with boiling water. While they soak, make a thick béchamel sauce (see below). Clean the fresh mushrooms and slice thin. Lift the dried mushrooms out of the bowl, chop them, and sauté with the fresh mushrooms in the rest of the butter. Season with salt and pepper, and when nearly cooked, add the garlic and parsley. Add the sauce to the mushrooms and taste. If needed, strain in more mushroom liquor.

Béchamel Sauce

Melt 1 tablespoon butter in a saucepan. Stir in the flour and cook gently for a few minutes. Warm the broth and cream separately, and whisk into the flour and butter. Season lightly with salt, pepper, and nutmeg. Add 2–3 tablespoons of the mushroom soaking liquid, being careful not to disturb any sand that has settled to the bottom of the bowl. (The strength of the mushroom liquor will vary; add it to taste.) Simmer the sauce for 30 minutes or so.

Cook the pasta and add it to the mushroom sauce; taste and correct seasoning. Put the pasta in a buttered gratin dish and top with grated cheese. Bake for about 15 minutes, until the top is crusty and golden.

Serves 4.

Goddess of Transcendental Anger's Hot'n' Spicy Mango Curry

Meera Vaidyanathan

This recipe is modified from one of Madhur Jaffrey's many cookbooks. Madhur, of course, does not dedicate the curry to the goddess of transcendental anger—that was Sara Lerner's idea!

3 medium ripe mangoes
1 teaspoon ground turmeric
1 teaspoon cayenne pepper
1–1½ teaspoons salt
2 ounces brown sugar (optional)
11 ounces coconut, freshly grated
3–4 fresh hot green chillies, coarsely chopped
½ tablespoon cumin seeds
½ pint yogurt, lightly beaten
2 tablespoons vegetable oil
½ teaspoon mustard seeds
3–4 dried hot red chillies, broken into halves
½ teaspoon fenugreek seeds
10–12 fresh curry leaves (for garnish)

Peel, pit, and cut the mangoes into 1" pieces. Put the mangoes in a medium-sized pan and add 1 cup of water. Cover and stew for 8–10 minutes over medium-low heat, stirring occasionally. Add the turmeric, cayenne pepper, and salt. Stir well. (If you prefer a sweeter curry or if the mangoes are more tart than sweet, add the brown sugar.)

Place coconut, green chillies, and cumin seeds in a blender, and add up to 1 cup water. Blend to make a fine paste.

When the mangoes are cooked, mash them to a pulp. Add the coconut paste. Mix.

Cover and simmer over medium heat, stirring occasionally, until the mixture becomes thick, about 10–15 minutes.

Then fold in the yogurt and continue cooking, still stirring, until just warmed through. Do not let the mixture come to the boil.

Remove from the heat and put aside. Check for seasoning.

Heat oil in a small saucepan over a medium-high heat. When hot, add mustard seeds. When the mustard seeds begin to pop (a matter of a few seconds), add the chillies, fenugreek seeds, and curry leaves. Stir-fry for a few seconds more, until the chillies darken (but do not allow to blacken). Quickly add the contents of the small pan to the mangoes. Stir to mix.

Serves 4–6. Serve with rice or rotis.

Main (Dis)Courses III

Frying Leviathan

Fish & Seafood Dishes

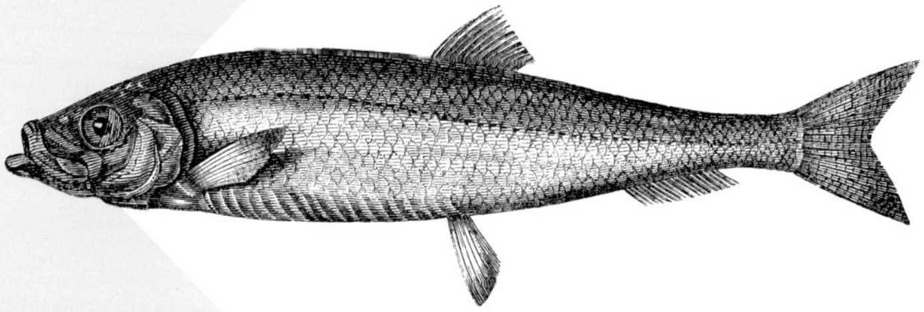

The Universe in a Trout Cake

Ingrid Gnerlich

This makes 4 trout cakes (for 2 people), but you can easily double or triple it, if you have more people to feed.

⅓ cup mayonnaise
¾ teaspoon Old Bay seasoning
8 ounces cooked trout, broken into chunks
⅓ cup breadcrumbs
¼ cup minced green onions or scallions
¼ cup minced red bell pepper

Mix everything together; try to avoid breaking up the trout too much. Form mixture into 4 patties, ½-inch thick each. Place an additional ⅓ cup of breadcrumbs into a shallow bowl. Press the cakes into the crumbs, coating completely. Remove cakes, and fry them in olive oil over medium heat, 6 minutes per side, or until brown and crisp.

Serve with lemon or lime wedges, or hot pepper sauce, or whatever you think best. Also good with catfish or tilapia, if you didn't have any luck catching a few trout!

Not for Resale Sunshine Kabobs Galleys

Jessica Pellien

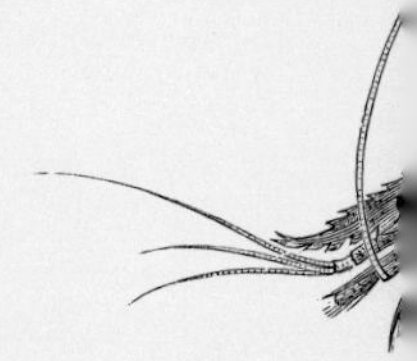

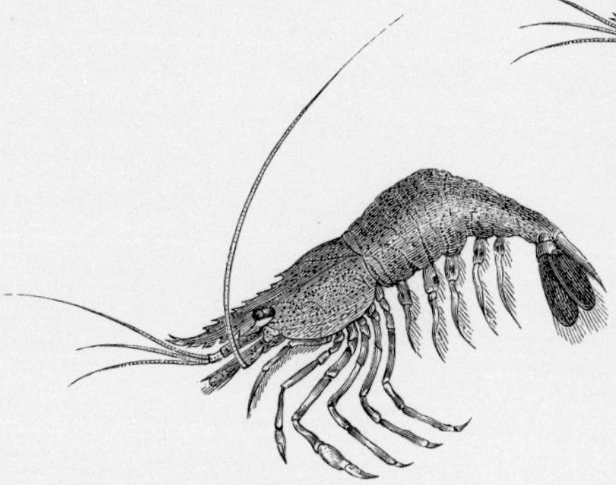

KABOBS
1 pound large shrimp (approx. 20 pieces), shelled
2–3 yellow squash, chopped into large chunks
1 large Vidalia onion, cut into sixths
½ fresh pineapple, chopped into large chunks

MARINADE
3 tablespoons fish sauce
¼ cup lime juice
¼ cup honey
1½ tablespoons fresh ginger, grated
a pinch red pepper flakes
salt and pepper to taste

Whisk all ingredients for the marinade together and pour over shrimp in a bowl. Cover bowl with plastic wrap and refrigerate for 30–45 minutes. Assemble kebobs with even distribution of shrimp, squash, onion, and pineapple. Grill for 15 minutes, turning frequently and basting with remaining marinade.

Serve over rice.

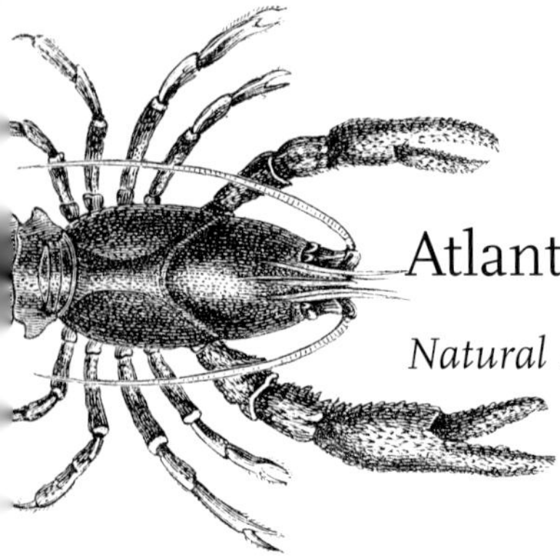

Atlantic Shorelines

Natural History and Lobster Rolls

Seth Ditchik

Though we love our little central New Jersey life, there are a few things we find ourselves missing about Massachusetts, where we lived prior to moving here. That list would include the Boston Red Sox, Cape Ann, the buskers on Harvard Square, and last, but certainly not least, a good lobstah roll. Following is my wife's adaptation of this traditional New England delicacy; enjoy!

1 pound cooked, picked fresh lobster meat (or equivalent fresh or defrosted jumbo lump crabmeat)
1 cup heavy cream
1 tablespoon butter
¼ cup finely diced shallots
¼ cup finely diced red pepper
¼ cup finely diced, seeded plum tomato
a big pinch each of: chopped parsley; picked or chopped dill; chopped thyme (this works out to about 1–2 tablespoons each—or less if you prefer a more Spartan approach to seasoning)
salt and pepper, to taste
lemon, squirt to taste
rolls, according to social venue

Pick through shellfish, and then again, for shells, taking care not to break up large chunks. Set aside in a medium-sized prep bowl. Sweat the shallots in butter. Let cool and add to the shellfish with the red pepper, tomato, and herbs.

Meanwhile, reduce the cream to ½ cup (or so); let cool, and add to the shellfish mix. Season everything lightly with salt and white pepper. If it's lacking a certain je ne sais quois, add a squirt (or 2) of lemon juice to perk it up.

Tradition demands that lobster rolls are served on cheap, split-top hot dog buns; they would do better on nice buttered and toasted brioche rolls (Come on! You're eating heavy cream! What's a little more butter and eggs?) Dress rolls with some mâche* or good mesclun. Serve with nice fries on the side. The Puritans would disapprove mightily.

Serves as many as you could offer in good conscience—as little as two, as many as four.

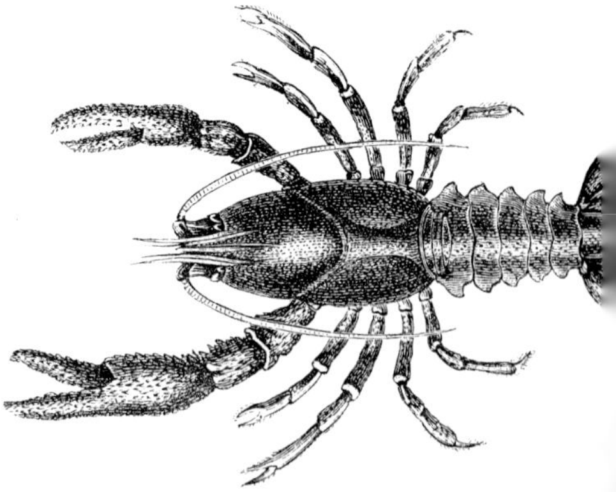

*Mâche is the secret formula for Red Sox Nation machismo.

Sensuous Seas Scallops

Intuitive and Intrinsic Approaches to Spiciness

Kathy Cioffi

This dish can be made with the streetwalkers of the scallop world—cheap, frozen, small bay scallops—and it's pretty good, but high-class, expensive call-girl scallops (aka fresh sea scallops) are much better, of course.

1 small onion (or ½ large one)
1 clove garlic
1 tablespoon canola (or other vegetable) oil
1 teaspoon curry powder
2 bay leaves
1 cup dry white wine
1 pound scallops (defrosted, if you're using frozen ones)
2 tablespoons white flour
½ cup water

Chop the onion and mince the garlic. Heat the canola oil in a medium-sized skillet, and then sauté the onion and garlic until the onion is soft.

Add the curry powder to the skillet and sauté for another minute, while stirring constantly. Add the bay leaves, wine, and scallops to the skillet, bring to a boil, lower the heat to simmer, cover the skillet, and cook for another 5 minutes or so. (Don't overcook! If you use small bay scallops, you may need less time, but large sea scallops may need a minute or so longer.)

Check to see if the scallops are opaque. If they are, remove them from the skillet, using a slotted spoon, and put them in a covered dish to keep them warm; add most of the onion-garlic mixture to the covered dish as well. Remove the bay leaves and throw them away.

Mix the flour and water together. Pour the flour-water mixture into a heated skillet while stirring with a whisk. When the liquid has thickened (this only takes a minute or so), pour it over the scallops in the covered dish.

Et voilà!

You have a tasty, mildly spicy fish dish that yields 4 servings.

I like to serve it with shahi pilau rice (available from Cinnabar Foods as a mix), and a yogurt-cucumber-tomato-scallion salad.

Prawn-tastic Seafood Paella

Tractatus with Monism on the Half-shell — Rob Tempio

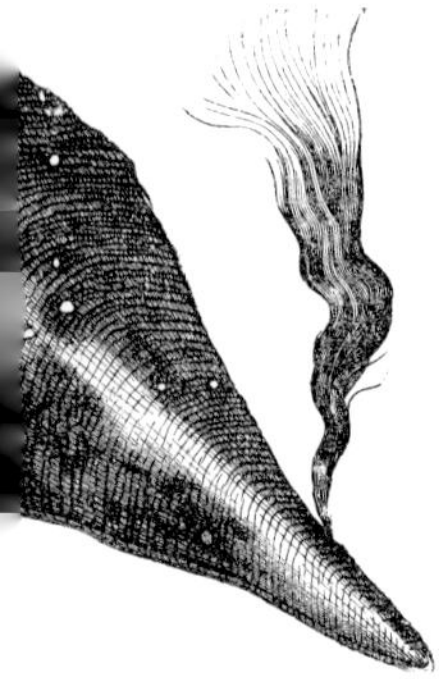

This recipe may read like the index from one of Robert Kirk's Field Guides to Crustaceans, *but don't let that deter you. Just dig in and enjoy. You won't be disappointed. My wife Erin made this for a dinner party we had and all the guests agreed that it's prawn-tastic!*

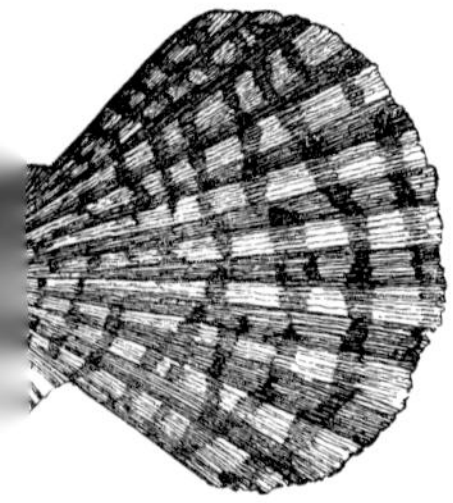

- 1 red bell pepper, sliced
- 1 cup frozen green peas
- ½ cup olive oil
- 1 whole chicken, cut into pieces
- ¼ pound of prosciutto, diced
- ½ pound chorizo or garlic sausage, sliced
- 1 pork chop, boned and diced
- 1 pound medium shrimp, shelled and deveined
- 1 large onion, chopped
- 1 cup chopped scallions
- 4 garlic cloves, sliced
- 2 cups short-grain white rice
- 1 cup long-grain wild rice
- 1 quart chicken stock
- ½ teaspoon saffron threads
- 1 tablespoon fresh lemon juice
- 2 bay leaves
- 8 prawns
- 1 pound cockles (preferably from New Zealand—just ask Sam Elworthy to send you some)
- 1 pound mussels
- sea salt, to taste
- ground black pepper, to taste

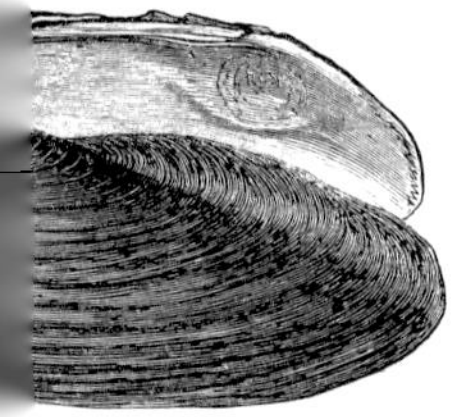

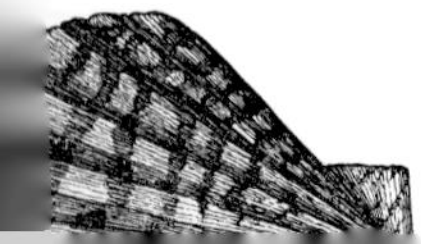

Char the red pepper over a gas flame or under a broiler. When cooled, rinse away the seeds and charred skin; dice the pepper.

Heat the olive oil in a cast-iron skillet. Brown the chicken pieces over medium-high heat. When they are golden on all sides, remove from the oil and sprinkle them with sea salt and ground black pepper. Add the prosciutto, chorizo, and pork to the skillet and brown for 5–10 minutes.

Bring the chicken broth to a boil and add the saffron threads.

Put the red pepper, chicken, prosciutto, chorizo, pork, onion, bay leaves, lemon juice, scallions, and garlic in a slow cooker and fill with the saffron broth.

Cook on high for 4 hours.

Pour boiling water over the green peas to defrost. Add the peas and shrimp to the slow cooker and cook on low for another ½ hour. Boil the prawns in a pot of water until they are bright red.

Steam the cockles and mussels in a pot until the shells open (about 10 minutes).

Cook separately the white rice and the wild rice; place a layer of each onto dinner plates. Spoon the meats and broth from the slow cooker over the rice; add the cockles and mussels.

Top with a prawn and serve.

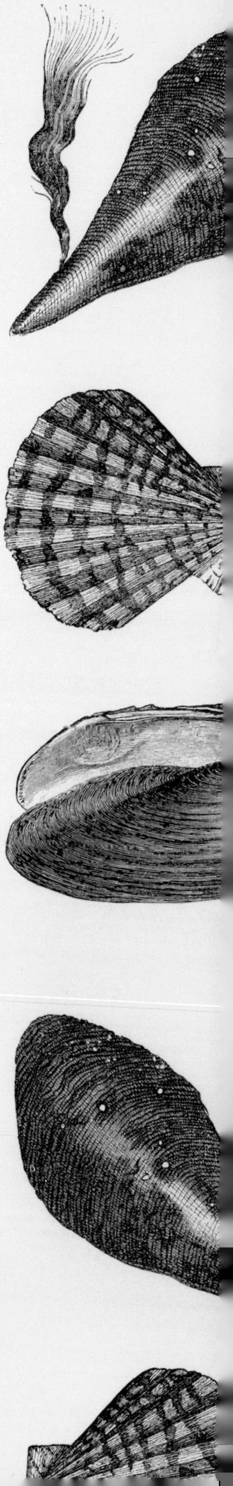

A Century in Cooks

A Very Select List of

Princeton Classics

The Bollingen Martini

Herbert S. Bailey, Jr.

If you have trouble remembering how to pronounce "Bollingen," think of the Bollingen martini. The "o" is pronounced as in "olive," but there is no "gin" in a Bollingen martini ("ng" is pronounced as in "sing"). Hence, Bälingen. Bollingen is the Swiss village where C. G. Jung built his retreat.

2 ounces vodka*
¼ ounce driest possible sauterne
3 drops Campbell's ambrosia†
1 olive, small (takes less room)

Combine ingredients and stir on the rocks or standing up. Sip slowly, with good conversation. After 2 or 3 of these, whatever you have for dinner, you will have wonderful dreams.

We offer this recipe in honor of Jack Barrett, editor of Bollingen Series, and in memory of Vaun Gillmor, the assistant editor. We drink to them.

*See Vladimir Nabokov's translation of Pushkin's *Eugene Onegin*, vol. 1, chap. 6, stanza xxi, line 14. (Bollingen Series LXXII, 2d ed., Princeton, 1975.)

†Possibly an allusion to a discussion of ambrosia in *The Hero with a Hundred Faces*, one of J. Campbell's lesser offerings (Rinky-Dink Potato Press, 2008, p.163): "The supreme boon desired for the Indestructible Body is uninterrupted residence in the Paradise of the Milk that Never Fails.... It is obvious that the infantile fantasies which we all cherish ... play continually into myth, fairy tale, and the teachings of the church, as symbols of indestructible being."

If Campbell's ambrosia is not readily obtainable at your local grocer's, we recommend substituting three drops of evaporated skim milk. [Ed.]

Backlist Boerenjongens

Or Dutch Courage

Loren Hoekzema

John de Witt, Grand Pensionary of Holland, probably enjoyed this liqueur sometime after 1625 but before 1672. De Witt played a vital and constructive role in Dutch affairs of state, but was the leading opponent of the House of Orange. When Prince William† came to power, public opinion turned against de Witt, and he and his brother Cornelius were hacked to death, with their limbs strung up on lamp posts by an angry mob.*

1 pound raisins
2 cups water
1 cinnamon stick
1 cup sugar
2 cups brandy

Simmer raisins, water, and cinnamon approximately 20 minutes. Add sugar and brandy, stirring until sugar is dissolved. Place mixture in sterilized containers. Seal. Let stand 3 months.

*We know this much from *John de Witt, Grand Pensionary of Holland, 1653–1672*, ed. G. Peyl; English translation by H. H. Rowan published by Princeton University Press in 1978.

†This was prior to, and very possibly the rationale for, the naming of Princeton, and the University's subsequent choice of orange as heraldic color; by coincidence, the prestigious Princeton University Press is located on a street named in the Prince's honor. [Ed.]

Clam Snacks

Florence Slade

1 8-ounce jar Old English Sharp cheese
½ stick (¼ cup) butter or margarine*
1 8-ounce can minced clams (drained)
1 package English muffins (6)
1–2 dashes Worcestershire sauce

Prepare in Advance

Melt butter and cheese in saucepan on low heat. Stir in clams, and add Worcestershire sauce. Split muffins open and place on cookie sheet or low pan; spread clam mixture over muffin halves. Place muffins and toppings in a freezer bag (or bread wrapper). Freeze. When hardened, remove and cut each half muffin into 4 pieces (24 pieces), and refreeze until needed.

To Serve

Preheat oven to 375 degrees (F).

Take as many muffins as desired directly from freezer and bake on a sheet or low pan (greased) for 15 minutes.

*O. H. Brownlees's pamphlet on the virtues of margarine was published in 1943 by Iowa State University Press, despite attempts by the butter industry to have it supressed. Big Butter's campaign to halt publication was resisted successfully by then Press Director Harold Ingle, although the case almost slipped out of his hands.

Marginalia

Salads, Sauces &
Savory Puddings

Red-Breasted Boiled Beets

Sam Elworthy

IDENTIFICATION: Key identification features are two large red mounds protruding from white gunk. Subspecies *Parsilia* features spots of green on top. Juveniles are smaller. Geriatrics are larger and tougher.

RANGE: Long assumed extinct after last confirmed sighting in its native New Zealand in 1954, but recently there have been unconfirmed reports of Red-Breasted Boiled Beets in Lambertville, New Jersey.

BEHAVIOR: White gunk and red breasts occasionally merge into pink mush on arrival at table. Red boiling liquid has been known to produce startling red stains on floors, clothes, and faces, etc.

BEETS
8 medium-sized beets
parsley, for garnish

WHITE SAUCE
1 stick of butter (½ cup)
4 tablespoons flour
¼ teaspoon salt
2 cups milk

BEETS

Boil beets until you can poke a fork in them—around 45 minutes. Drain beets, run them under cold water, and use a knife to take off skin and trim the ends.

WHITE SAUCE

Melt butter on medium heat, add flour, and mix; add salt, and then add milk slowly, while stirring vigorously. Sauce should be thick but not solid—add more milk if too thick, weep if too thin, and proceed anyway.

Put 2 beets on each plate. Pour white sauce on top. Garnish with parsley.

Eat!

Serves 4 people.

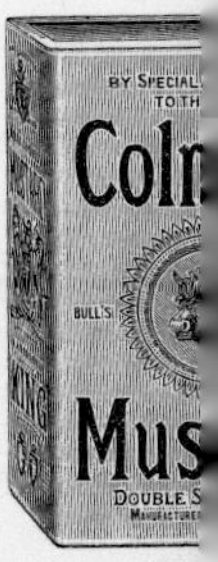

Creative Destruction Cabbage

Mom's Thanksgiving Cole Slaw

Peter Dougherty

Peter remembers this as a special holiday preparation (back when slicing cabbage was not automated); he came up with his mother's handwritten recipe on a card dated "11-21-82"—received just in time to carry on a family Thanksgiving tradition that year. We've transcribed it as follows:

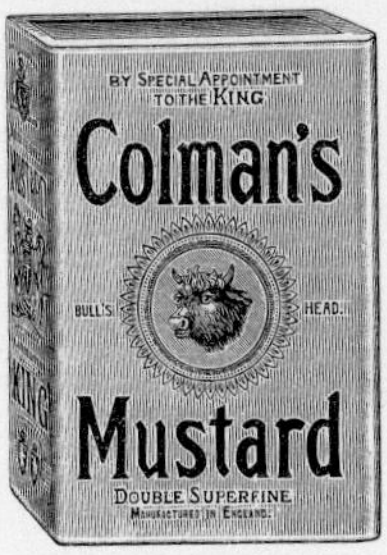

SLAW

1 green cabbage, sliced "as thin as possible"

mustard powder (a "generous sprinkle")

SAUCE

4–5 eggs

1 cup milk (no doubt whole)

½ cup vinegar (white)

½ cup sugar

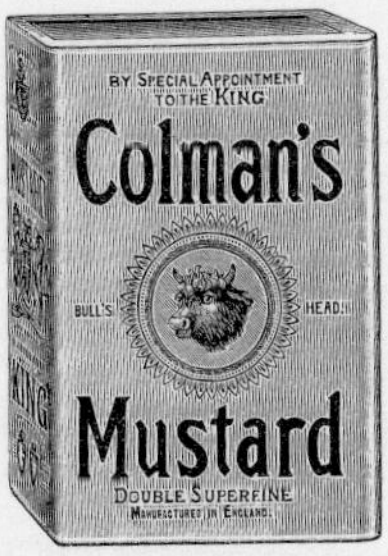

Season sliced cabbage with mustard; toss; set aside. Combine sauce ingredients over a low flame, stirring constantly, until mixture becomes "custard-like." Remove from flame, and add to slaw. Toss gently, and serve.

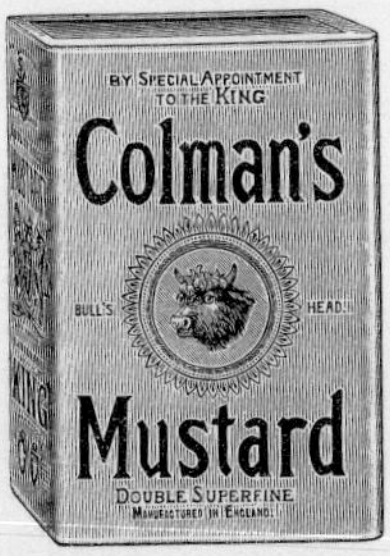

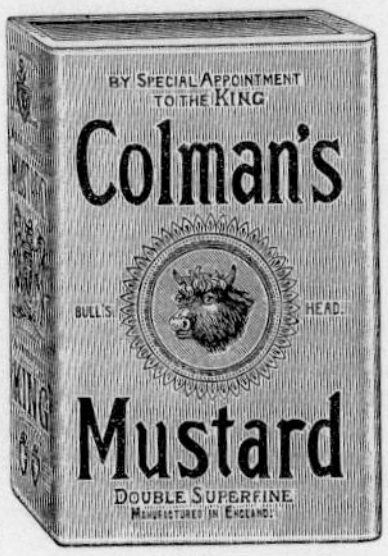

New French Thought and Word Salad Niçoise

From My Grand'mère

Victoria Hansard

This recipe comes from my French mother-in-law.

SALAD

4 large boiling potatoes (cooked 20 minutes, peeled and cut into bite-size pieces)
1½ pounds green beans (cooked 15 minutes)
red onion (chopped)
1 8-ounce can tuna in oil
2 medium tomatoes (chopped)
2 hard-boiled eggs (chopped)
8 black Greek olives, pitted
2 tablespoons chopped chives or scallion tips

DRESSING

¾ cup olive oil
¼ cup red wine vinegar
¼ cup finely chopped herbs: parsley, chives, tarragon, and basil
salt and pepper to taste

Mix all salad ingredients. Combine dressing ingredients. Toss salad, with dressing.

Serve with warm French bread and a chilled white wine.

Compelling Need Taco Salad

Mary Ellis

1 pound ground beef or turkey
1 package of taco seasoning
1 jar of salsa
2 8-ounce packages cream cheese, softened
1 8-ounce package shredded cheddar cheese
lettuce, shredded

Brown ground beef/turkey in oiled saucepan; add packet of taco seasoning. Set aside to cool. Spread out softened cream cheese on a large platter; then spread ground beef/turkey on top of cream cheese layer. Add a few tablespoons of salsa on top. Add shredded lettuce. Add the cheddar cheese. Top off with a few more tablespoons of salsa.

If preparing a day ahead, do not add the final layer of salsa until ready to serve.

Betsnaise Coordinating Sauce

Betsy Litz

6 ounces unsalted butter
2 shallots, chopped
1 teaspoon dried tarragon
1 teaspoon dried chervil
¼ teaspoon ground pepper
2 tablespoons tarragon vinegar
2 tablespoons dry white wine
2 egg yolks

Melt the butter in a small pan over low heat. Remove from the heat. In another small saucepan, combine the shallots, tarragon, chervil, pepper, vinegar, and wine. Bring to a boil over moderately high heat, until the liquid is reduced to only 1 teaspoon. Add the egg yolks and 2 tablespoons of water to the reduction of spices, and whisk constantly over moderate heat until thick and fluffy (2–3 minutes). As soon as the sauce is thick enough that you can't see the bottom of the pan, remove from the heat. Continue whisking for several seconds. Let the mixture cool for a minute. Then, whisking continually, slowly add the melted butter (this should be no hotter than the egg yolks). Season with salt to taste.

You may keep the sauce warm in a double boiler over warm water for up to an hour before serving.

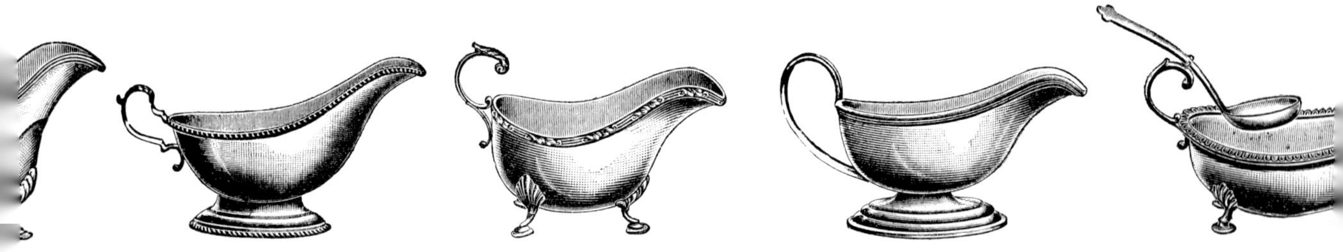

Where the Two Came to Their Blender

The Presence of Walnuts in the Techniques of Ecstacy Margaret Case

This easy sauce is delicious on vegetables, rice, tofu—just about anything. It keeps very well in the refrigerator.

2 cups apple juice
2 cups walnuts
½ cup miso paste
1 tablespoon chopped fresh ginger root, or more to taste
1 tablespoon cider vinegar

Heat apple juice; when it boils, turn it off. Add miso paste, whisking to dissolve (lumps may remain). Place walnuts and ginger in bowl of blender, add miso mixture, and blend thoroughly. Add vinegar and blend.

Yield: about 4 cups.

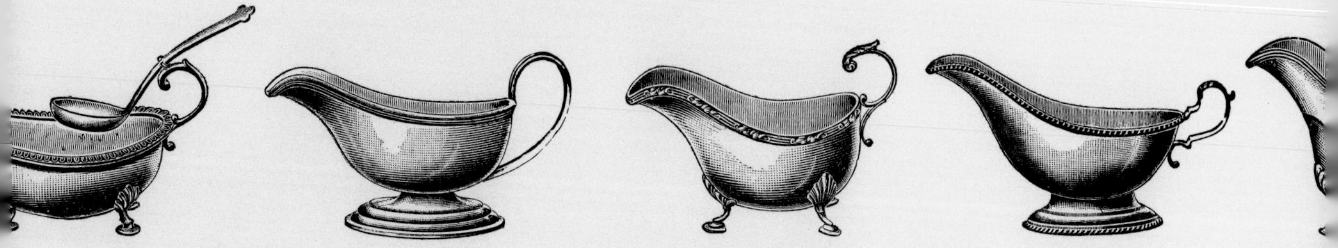

Contested Sauce for Economics Majors at Liberal Arts Colleges

Nutrition and the Prisoner's Dilemma

William Chang

This sauce was handed down to me at a most crucial point in my life: when I was a starving undergrad. This is a hearty sauce and a hearty meal and will provide a large amount of energy for the scholar in all of us.

1 pound ground beef
2 cloves chopped garlic
½ cup chopped carrots
1 cup chopped white onions
½ cup chopped celery
1 28-ounce can tomato sauce (canned sauce is cheaper, but jar sauce works just fine)
1 tablespoon red wine, or to taste (chef recommends ½ cup Pinot Noir)
1 tablespoon salt
pasta
olive oil
1 teaspoon double-concentrate tomato paste

In a large pot add enough olive oil to coat the bottom of the pot and let sit on high flame for 10 seconds. Now add to pot the chopped garlic, carrots, onions, and celery. Lightly brown vegetables—the aromatics of the vegetables should be a sign that it is time to add the ground beef.

Upon adding the beef to the pot, use a wooden spoon to break the beef up. (As the beef browns it should get a lot easier. You do not want the beef to clump up.) When all the ground beef is broken up, add the tablespoon of red wine. The adventurous can add more. Does the type of wine matter? Absolutely not, but I recommend the Pinot Noir (it gives the sauce a certain full-bodied kick).

It is important to add the wine before the tomato sauce, otherwise you will have a very soupy, wine flavored sauce. Stir the wine, beef, and vegetables until the wine evaporates.

When the wine is soaked up, add the tomato sauce. Stir a bit, and let pot of sauce sit on medium heat. (The longer you cook it, the thicker the sauce.) Once the sauce is simmering, add the teaspoon of tomato paste.

Throughout this whole process you should be checking, stirring, and tasting the meat sauce. Add salt as required. The sauce will normally be ready in 30–45 minutes.

Which pasta should you boil and serve with this?

I prefer either spaghetti or a thinner, longer pasta, but the Invisible Hand will dictate selection. Whatever the choice: once the water has come to a boil, add a tablespoon of salt to the water. Pasta loses much of its salt content in the boiling process, and this helps to restore the taste.

I hope you enjoy my meat sauce!
Serves 4, or 2 of me.

Triumph of the Yorkshire Pudding

"Blad Pudding," for You Yanks

Richard Baggaley

Worth explaining that this is not a sweet pudding— but rather something you would traditionally eat with roast beef. For the best effect you really also need lashings of lovely gravy to pour onto (or better still, into, if it has risen nicely) your Yorkshire pud.

3 ounces plain flour
1 egg
5 ounces full-fat milk
salt
freshly milled black pepper
2 teaspoons sunflower oil

Preheat oven to 220 degrees (C), 425 degrees (F), or gas mark 7.

To make the batter, sift the flour into a bowl and make a well in the centre. Break an egg into the well and beat it in, gradually incorporating the flour, milk, and seasoning (I would use an electric hand-whisk). Heat oil in oven in a 28 x 18-cm or 11 x 7-inch roasting tin until very hot. Pour the mixed batter into the sizzling oil and cook on the top shelf of the oven. The pudding will take 25–30 minutes to rise and become crisp and golden. Serve at once with roast beef, gravy, and horseradish sauce.

Serves 4.

Kugel's Noodle Ladder Pudding Pie

Fred Appel

A variation on the noodle puddings my mom used to make. Good for lunch with a salad, or as a side dish.

½ bag (6 ounces) egg noodles, medium size
2 onions, chopped
3 tablespoons oil
2 eggs, lightly beaten
1 carrot, grated
⅓ cup raisins
salt and pepper, or curry powder—or spice of choice

Boil salted water in saucepan for the noodles. Add noodles and cook just until soft. Meanwhile, heat 2 tablespoons oil in 10- to 12-inch nonstick frying pan. Fry onions with a pinch of salt until soft and brown. Drain noodles; mix in eggs, grated carrot, raisins, spices, and onions. Heat 1 tablespoon oil in frying pan; pour in noodle mixture and fry, without stirring, until it's brown on the bottom. Flip. (Slide noodle disc onto a large plate, cover with another large plate, and flip over; slide flipped noodle disc back into pan.) Fry other side.

Cultural Contradictions in Continuous Bok Choy Salad

Charlene Borsack

Make dressing at least one hour ahead of time. I usually cover and place in the refrigerator for a chilled dressing, but it can be left at room temperature.

Dressing
3 tablespoons soy sauce
⅓ cup white vinegar
½ cup sugar
½ cup canola oil

Salad
1–2 bunches bok choy, chopped
1 bunch scallions, chopped
¾ cup slivered almonds (I toast them in the oven on a cookie sheet; let them cool and then add to salad)
¾ cup unsalted sunflower seeds
1 package ramen noodles, uncooked (discard flavor packet)

Dressing

Combine dressing ingredients and allow dressing to sit for at least one hour.

Salad

Combine salad ingredients and toss. Pour the dressing over the salad and gently toss a little bit more.

Modifying Complexities in Simple Avocado-Tomato Salad

Maria Lindenfeldar

Here's my favorite avocado-tomato salad, courtesy of Jacques Pepin—simplified and altered by me.

SALAD
2 ripe avocados (cut in cubes)
1½ cups grape tomatoes (cut in half)
1 small red onion (sliced into thin half-moons)

VINAIGRETTE
1½ tablespoons red wine vinegar
2 tablespoons good olive oil

SEASONING
¼ teaspoon salt
¼ teaspoon ground pepper
4 drops Tabasco sauce

Place avocados, tomatoes, and red onion in a medium bowl. Drizzle vinaigrette on top and stir to combine. Add salt, pepper, and Tabasco sauce. Stir again.

Serve right away. Makes about 5 cups of salad. Sounds too simple to be that good, but it really is.

Wittgenstein Reads BBQ Marinade, with Tabasco and Liquid Smoke Amplifications

Diane Roth

This is not your average soy sauce marinade. At least, it's the best one I've ever made! The Liquid Smoke and Tabasco sauce give it a little extra zing!

¼ cup chopped onion
½ cup oil
¼ cup lemon juice
½ teaspoon pepper
2 tablespoons soy sauce
½ cup ketchup
¼ cup brown sugar
1 teaspoon dry mustard
dash Tabasco sauce
dash Liquid Smoke

Mix all these ingredients together. Poke a lot of holes in the meat, cover with sauce, and marinate for 24 hours. Then grill or broil to your liking.

I recommend this for a London broil.

Flour & Plenty

Breads, Muffins & Cookies

Irish Soda Bread after the Age of Joyce

Erin Suydam

4 cups unbleached flour
1 teaspoon baking soda
1 teaspoon salt
1 cup sugar
1 teaspoon caraway seeds
1 cup raisins
¾ cup butter (unsalted)
1 ⅓ cups buttermilk, plus extra for brushing

Preheat oven to 350 degrees (F).

In a large bowl, stir together flour, baking soda, salt, sugar, and caraway seeds. Make a well in the center. Melt butter (in the microwave or on the stovetop), add the buttermilk, and pour into well. Mix thoroughly, adding raisins while stirring, until a soft dough forms. Transfer dough to a floured surface and knead until smooth (1–2 minutes). Add a bit of flour if dough is sticky. Form dough into a ball and transfer to a lightly greased baking sheet. With a sharp knife, cut a cross into the top of the dough (about ½-inch deep, stopping 1 inch from the edges). With a small brush, brush some buttermilk onto the surface where the cross was cut. Place uncovered in oven and bake for 60–75 minutes (ovens vary), until the bread is golden brown. At about the halfway point, brush on some more buttermilk. Remove from the oven, cool thoroughly, slice, and enjoy.

A Banana Loaf of Their Own

When They Severed Earth from Canada

Valerie Ambrose

1 cup mashed bananas (3 medium)
⅓ cup* oil or melted butter
½ cup brown sugar
2 eggs, beaten
1¾ cup whole wheat flour
½ teaspoon salt
1 teaspoon baking soda
¼ cup hot water

Preheat oven to 325 degrees (F).

In a large bowl, beat together oil and brown sugar. Add eggs; mix well. Stir in mashed bananas. Sift together dry ingredients. Add these and hot water, alternately, to banana mixture. Mix batter until smooth. Pour into greased 9 x 5 x 3-inch loaf pan, and bake for 55–60 minutes. Cool on wire rack for ½ hour before slicing.

Freezes well.

* Note for Canadians: Many apologies for the nonmetric measurements. Substitute poutine for baking oil. Serve with a side of maple syrup and fake bacon. To cool, place loaf outside igloo window for 5 seconds. To freeze loaf, place outside igloo window for 30 seconds. Do not overfreeze.

The Evolution of Maia's Complexity Mango-Cranberry Nut Bread

Maia Reim

This is a recipe I concocted when I had lots of ripe mangoes I wanted to use up. To make 1 cup of mango pulp you will probably need 2 large mangoes, but the exact amount is not critical—applesauce or mashed bananas, or whatever you have to work with, can be substituted for mangoes.

½ cup skim, soy, almond, or rice milk, blended with
  2 teaspoons vinegar to make "buttermilk"
½ cup canola oil
1 cup puréed mango pulp
1 cup sugar (I like to use brown sugar for ¼ of this)
2 eggs (or ½ cup Eggbeaters)
1 teaspoon vanilla extract
1 teaspoon almond extract
1¾ cups flour
¼ cup wheat germ or bran
½ teaspoon salt
1 teaspoon baking soda
1½ teaspoons baking powder
1 teaspoon cinnamon (optional)
½ cup chopped walnuts
¾ cup chopped raw cranberries or raisins
2 tablespoons fresh grated citrus peel (optional)

Preheat oven to 350 degrees (F).

Blend together the milk, oil, mango pulp, sugar, eggs, vanilla extract, and almond extract. In separate large bowl, combine flour, wheat germ, baking soda, cinnamon, walnuts, cranberries, and citrus peel. Add liquid ingredients to the dry, and blend until just moistened. Pour into 2 medium-sized or one large greased loaf pan; bake in oven for 35 minutes, or until an inserted toothpick comes out clean.

Serves many. Freezes well. Makes great muffins too.

It is nice to keep one loaf at home and bring one to the kitchen at PUP.

Remote-Access Proofreading Scones

Heather Hansen

Good for eating while proofreading direct mail catalogs.

2 cups flour
3 tablespoons sugar
1 tablespoon baking powder
¼ teaspoon salt
6 tablespoons chilled butter
1 egg, beaten
½ cup plus an extra tablespoon half-and-half
2 tablespoons sugar

Preheat oven to 400 degrees (F).

Combine flour, sugar, baking powder, and salt. Cut in butter. Combine egg and half-and-half; add to dry mixture. Stir until moistened. Turn dough onto a floured surface. Knead until nearly smooth. Pat or lightly roll to ½-inch thickness. Cut with a 2½- or 3-inch cutter (I use an upside-down drinking glass). Place scones on an ungreased baking sheet. Brush tops with the extra tablespoon half-and-half, sprinkle with the extra 2 tablespoons sugar. Bake for 12–15 minutes until golden. Cool on a wire rack for 5 minutes; serve warm.

Makes 10–12 scones.

Princeton Field Guide to Carrot-Raisin Muffins

Ellen Foos

Recognition: Coloration highly variable but most commonly orange and black.
Occurrence: Infrequently in winter when guests are expected.
Remarks: A muffin tasty enough to kindle interest even in the picky eater.

1½ cups sugar (or less)
1 cup oil
3 large eggs, beaten
2 teaspoons vanilla extract
7-ounce can crushed pineapple, with juice
2 cups plus 2 tablespoons all-purpose flour
2 teaspoons baking soda
1½ teaspoons cinnamon
1 teaspoon salt
2 cups grated carrots
1 cup raisins
1 cup chopped nuts

Preheat oven to 375 degree (F).

In a medium-sized bowl, mix the first four ingredients and add the pineapple. In a large bowl, combine the flour, baking soda, cinnamon, and salt. Add the egg mixture and mix until moistened. The batter will be thick. Add grated carrots, raisins, and chopped nuts, if desired. Fill greased muffin cups ¾ full. Bake for 15–20 minutes.

Makes 2 dozen small or regular muffins, or 1 dozen Texas-size.

Spelt-Check Muffins with Apples and Carrots

Carmina Alvarez

This recipe does not use white flour or sugar, and it may require a special trip to the health-food store of your choice. The muffins are especially delicious to those health-conscious individuals who have discovered the joys of organic foods, stevia sweetener, and almond milk.

3 cups spelt flour
¾ cup flax meal
4 teaspoons stevia sweetener
1 cup raisins (or ½ cup raisins and ½ cup dried cranberries)
2 teaspoons baking soda
1 teaspoon baking powder
½ teaspoon salt
2 teaspoon cinnamon
1–2 teaspoons vanilla extract (I like 3)
4 eggs (from free-range chickens—they are happier)
¾ cup milk (I use organic almond milk—it's healthier)
4 apples, shredded or cut into small cubes
1½ cups shredded carrots
1 cup nuts of your choice (optional)
lots of love and gratitude

Preheat oven to 350 degrees (F).

It's easier to mix all the dry ingredients in one bowl, and all the liquid ones in another; then mix all together—the mixture will look "funny." Important: do this with love and gratitude (you can really taste it later on) for all the healthy, organic ingredients you are using.

Pour into muffin cups. Bake for about 20 minutes. The muffins should look golden and be hard to the touch—then you'll know they are ready (it may take more than 20 minutes in the oven).

Makes about a dozen large muffins.
Enjoy!

Martha Mahood's Delicious Orange Cookies

The Zest in the Golden Vase

Frank Mahood

My mother made these all my life, and now that she's gone, there is only my nephew, Kevin, who continues to make them.

COOKIES
¾ cup margarine or Crisco
¾ cup sugar
2 eggs
6 tablespoons fresh-squeezed orange juice
2 cups flour
2 teaspoons baking powder
1 teaspoon baking soda
orange rind (for zest; save a little for the frosting!)

FROSTING
½ box powdered sugar
1 tablespoon butter
dash of reserved orange zest
a small amount of orange Juice

COOKIES

Preheat oven to 375 degrees (F).

In a mixing bowl, combine and thoroughly mix all ingredients except the orange zest. Finely grate the orange rind to create the zest. (Note: This is the tricky part! You want to add only a bit, to give the cookies added orange flavor, and mix some flecks of orange into the cookies, but how much you use depends on your taste—experiment!) Place batter on a greased cookie sheet in globs—roughly 2" in diameter and ½" thick (this is a guess), and bake for 8–10 minutes. Allow cookies to cool before frosting.

FROSTING

The frosting is the necessary final touch. In a mixing bowl, combine thoroughly the powdered sugar and butter. Add (to taste) a bit of the left-over orange zest, just enough orange juice to make the frosting thick and creamy. Spread over baked cookies.

Rational Choice Oatmeal Chocolate Chip Cookies*

Chuck Myers

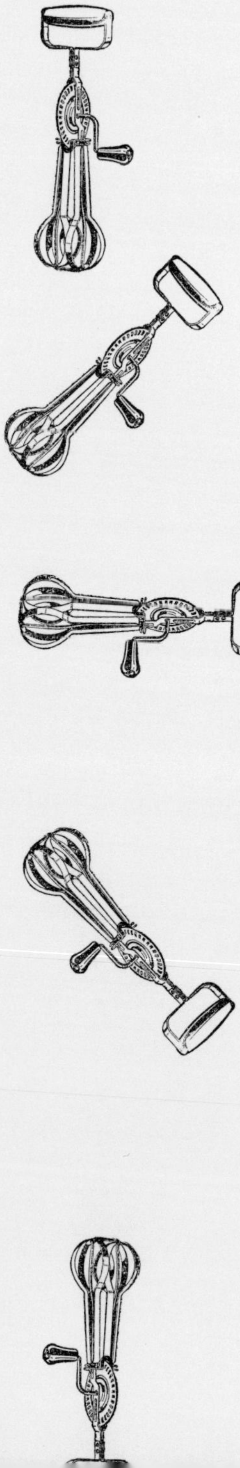

I've made these cookies for my kids for many years. They were a great hit, I'm told, at cookie sales for various high school fundraisers.

½ cup brown sugar
½ cup granulated sugar
½ cup butter
1 egg
1 teaspoon vanilla extract
1 tablespoon milk
1 cup all-purpose white flour
½ teaspoon baking powder
½ teaspoon baking soda
½ teaspoon salt
1 cup quick rolled oats
¾ cup chocolate chips

Preheat oven to 350 degrees (F).

Combine brown sugar, granulated sugar, and butter. Add egg, vanilla extract, and milk. In a separate bowl, mix together baking powder, baking soda, and salt. Combine the flour mixture and the butter-and-sugar mixture. Add in rolled oats and chocolate chips. On greased cookie sheets, bake in oven for about 10 minutes, or until gold in color.

*Adapted from *The Joy of Cooking.*

Mandel Brot

Adam Fortgang

3 eggs
¾ cup oil
1 cup sugar
2 cups flour
1 teaspoon baking powder
1 teaspoon vanilla extract
chopped walnuts and raisins—to taste;
    try a handful of each
grease for cookie sheets

Preheat oven to 350 degrees (F).

Mix eggs, sugar, oil, and flour thoroughly. Add chopped walnuts and raisins. Pour onto greased cookie sheet and bake until light brown—approximately 25 minutes. Remove from oven, loosen. Make 3 strips, about 3 x 12-inch apiece; slicing carefully. Return to oven for another 10 minutes, till brown.

Mandel Brot

3 eggs
¾ cup oil
1 cup sugar
2 cups flour
1 teaspoon baking powder
1 teaspoon vanilla extract
chopped walnuts and raisins—to taste;
    try a handful of each
grease for cookie sheets

Preheat oven to 350 degrees (F).

Mix eggs, sugar, oil, and flour thoroughly. Add chopped walnuts and raisins. Pour onto greased cookie sheet and bake until light brown—approximately 25 minutes. Remove from oven, loosen. Make 3 strips, about 3 x 12-inch apiece; slicing carefully. Return to oven for another 10 minutes, till brown.

Keirkegaard's Upbuilding Cookie Discourses

Linny Schenck

DANISH GINGERBIRDS
½ cup butter
¼ cup sugar
¼ cup light brown sugar
⅙ cup molasses
⅓ cup Karo light corn syrup
2¼ cup flour mixed with:
½ teaspoon baking soda
½ teaspoon salt
scant ¼ teaspoon ground cloves
½ tablespoon ginger
½ tablespoon cinnamon

Preheat oven to 350 degrees (F).

Cream butter separately and then add and cream the sugar until smooth. Add and beat in the molasses and light corn syrup. Sift flour together with the baking soda, salt, ginger, cloves and cinnamon before mixing into the butter-sugar-syrup mixture. Separate the dough into portions sized for reasonable handling. Pat each portion into thick patty. Chill dough. Then roll out and cut, using cookie cutters. Bake on cookie sheets for 8 minutes.

This is a very forgiving dough so it is great for holiday cooking with kids. The key is to form up your patties and let those chill well (overnight–or freeze for later rolling and cooking). Then, allow dough to warm slightly before handling again. If working with children, use lots of flour and roll out on wax paper to prevent sticking to work surface or rolling pin—the resulting cookies will be just a little tougher but the kids will have success with their gingerbread men and women!

Afterword

Moral Agents & Their Desserts

Cakes & Other Treats

The Theory of Corporate Trifle

Emma Green

1–1½ packets trifle sponges
4 ounces raspberries (or two tins)
2 tablespoons raspberry jam
1 pint custard (cold)
3 tablespoons sherry (or to taste)
½ pint double cream
cherries and chocolate sprinkles to decorate

Slice the trifle sponges into quarters and line them at the bottom of a glass trifle dish. Spread the raspberry jam over the sponge base and add sherry. Add raspberries. Pour the custard into the bowl and refrigerate until slightly set. Whisk cream until thick, then spread cream on top of custard layer. Chop cherries in half and arrange them on top of the cream like a clockface. Decorate with chocolate sprinkles. Refrigerate until ready to serve.

Serves 6–8.

Mythos Figs

Eustomachic Worship in Practice

Sara Lerner

I got this recipe from the cookbook The Ottoman Kitchen *by Sarah Woodward, where the figs were described as "Turkish Viagra." These divine figs are enough to intoxicate anyone.... If figured at one fig per person, this serves 12 (and obviously the recipe doubles easily).*

12 dried figs—they should be plump, still have their stems, and have unbroken skin
1 cup weak black tea, still warm
3 tablespoons honey
juice of ½ lemon
5 fresh bay leaves
12 walnuts, shelled and halved

Pour the warm tea over the figs and leave to soak overnight or for at least 5 hours.

Remove figs and make the liquid back up to 1 cup by adding fresh water. Pour liquid into a shallow pan in which all the figs will fit in one layer, but don't add the figs yet. To the liquid add the honey, lemon juice, and bay leaves. Bring this syrup to a boil, stirring continuously, and boil hard for 2 minutes; then reduce to a simmer.

Add figs, stem side up, and let simmer uncovered for 20 minutes, basting the figs occasionally with the syrup. Let cool in the syrup; when they're cool enough to handle, make a slit in each fig from the base of the stem, down a ways. Stuff 1 walnut half into each slit. Place figs in a serving dish and pour the syrup over., feel free to remove the bay leaves.

The figs will keep, even improve, for a day or two before serving.

On Demand Pear Pie with Lightning Topping

Debbie Tegarden

Assume a pie crust. I suggest buying the sort of folded-up, frozen crust that you can defrost and flop into a pie pan; once flopped, consider adding some artfully naïve indents with a fork. (It's between you and your conscience whether to present this as a homemade crust.)

Or you can use a frozen crust-in-a-pan, defrosted.

Moral absolutists are free to create a crust from scratch.

This recipe is designed for a 9-inch pan; deflate or inflate ingredient measures to adjust to other pie-pan sizes.

This is an autumn recipe, but it can be whipped up out of season by substituting canned pears and Craisins (unflavored) for the fresh fruit.

FILLING

6 large pears (or 8 little pears), peeled and chopped into ½-inch cubes (approx.), to yield about 3 cups
2½ cups cranberries (stemmed and rinsed)
½ cup brown sugar (packed)
½ cup white sugar
¼ cup all-purpose flour
1 teaspoon vanilla extract
½ teaspoon cinnamon

TOPPING

¼ cup all-purpose flour
⅓ cup chopped rolled oats (the "instant" oatmeal in the breakfast-cereal aisle)
¼ cup butter (use the real thing, if available)
¼ cup chopped walnuts (or, if you can, pecans)

FILLING

Preheat oven to 350 degrees (F).

Combine flour, brown and white sugar, vanilla extract, and cinnamon in a large bowl. Fold in cranberries and pear pieces, until well coated. Gently pour it all into your pie crust.

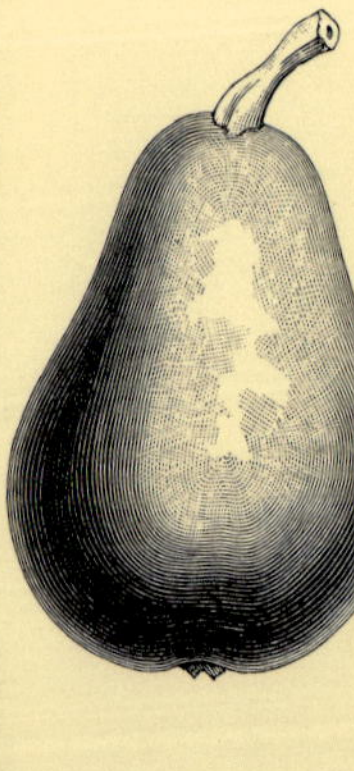

TOPPING

Combine flour, sugar, and oats. Cut in butter, using a chopper. (Lumpy is fine.) Add chopped nuts. Distribute topping deliberatively over pie filling. Cover pie-crust edges with aliminum foil. Bake for 25 minutes. Open oven and remove foil from crust's edges. Bake for another 30 minutes.

Serves about 8; excellent with frozen vanilla yogurt.

Grandma Rose's Insecure Prosperity Jewish Applecake

Homage à Ewa Morawska

Lauren Lepow

> Mom, this looks like an all-day project.
>
> —*Jean Irizarry*

oil, poppy seeds, and flour for preparing baking pan
6–8 large cooking apples
cinnamon sugar (to taste)
3 cups flour (plus additional flour to knead into dough)
2 teaspoons baking powder
½ cup sugar
pinch salt
1 stick margarine or butter, plus 3–4 tablespoons more to dot cake top
2 eggs
½ cup orange juice
jam or preserves (about 1 cup)
raisins (about 1 cup)
chopped walnuts (about 1 cup)
grated rind and juice of 1 lemon

Preheat oven to 350 degrees (F).

Oil bottom and sides of a large (about 10 x 15-inch) rectangular pan; dust with flour and sprinkle with poppy seeds.

Peel and slice apples and sprinkle with cinnamon sugar; set aside.

Prepare dough: in a large mixing bowl, mix flour, baking powder, sugar, and salt. Work margarine or butter into flour mixture. Make a well and drop in eggs and orange juice. Mix dough with a fork—it will be sticky. Turn out dough on a floured surface and knead in more flour until dough is of a consistency to be rolled out. Divide dough into three equal parts.

Assemble cake: roll out the first piece of dough and fit it into the pan. Put apple mixture on top of dough; add more cinnamon sugar, if desired. Roll out second piece of dough and fit it in over apples. Spread dough with jam or preserves; sprinkle on raisins, walnuts, lemon juice, lemon rind, and more cinnamon sugar. Roll out third piece of dough and fit it into the pan. Slice cake with sharp knife into small squares; dot with margarine or butter and sprinkle with cinnamon sugar. Bake for about 1½ hours (check for doneness after 1 hour).

Serves about 20, they should live and be well.

Zella Hoover's Mysterious Gypsy Apricot Tarts

Doctor Euler Never Had It This Good Vickie Kearn

My grandmother, Zella Hoover (named after a gypsy her father caught a fancy to) taught me how to make these tarts. No one really knows where she got the recipe. They take a while to make but are well worth it, as long as you don't have a cholesterol problem.

2 sticks butter
1 16-ounce package of cream cheese (the whipped stuff won't do)
2 cups flour
1 package dried apricots
powdered sugar

Put the dried apricots in a pot and slowly simmer, with as little water as possible. Please don't burn them because they smell awful and taste worse: you will have to keep an eye on them. While they are cooking, you can work on the dough.

Blend butter and cream cheese, and slowly add the flour (if you add it all at once you will have a big mess). I find it is easier to mix by hand; unless you are fortunate enough to have a dough hook, it is just too much for an electric beater to handle. Chill dough for one hour.

While the dough is chilling you can mash up your apricots and let them cool.

Preheat oven to 375 degrees (F).

Roll dough as thin as for a pie crust and cut into pieces about 3 inches square. Place a tablespoon of filling in the center of each, bring the points to the center, and press down slightly. (If you don't, the tarts will unfold while cooking; they will still taste great but won't be very pretty. Actually, you won't care what they look like they are so good.)

Bake on cookie sheets for 12 minutes or until lightly brown. Remove from oven and sift with powdered sugar over the tops, while warm.

If you don't like apricots, try your favorite preserves. Just make sure they are really thick.

Servings depend on how much you like these. I could eat them all myself. However, it usually makes 2 dozen tarts.

Strawberry Girl Shortcake

When Most Is Best

Daphne Ireland

This recipe is my mom's recipe; thanks, Lorraine Tams!

Every first week of June, my Strawberry Girl, Larissa, and I pick strawberries at a nearby farm—more accurately, I pick them and she "sneaks" them. There's nothing more irresistible than a sweet, sun-warmed strawberry, right off the stem. Same night, it's fresh Strawberry Girl Shortcake for dessert, which the boys, Gavin and Kent, love too.

2 cups flour
2 teaspoons baking powder
½ teaspoon salt
⅔ cup sugar
½ cup butter
⅔ cup milk
1 quart fresh or frozen strawberries (divided use)
⅔ cup light cream
1 teaspoon vanilla extract
sugar to taste
whipped cream (homemade is best, of course!)

Preheat oven to 425 degrees (F).

Sift together flour, baking powder, salt, and sugar. Cut in butter. Add milk. The batter will be thick, like biscuit dough. Spread into 2 buttered 9-inch cake pans. Bake for 10–12 minutes. Remove, and cool completely.

Meanwhile, blend ½ quart of strawberries (reserving other ½ quart for later use), cream, vanilla extract, and sugar to taste. Cut the leftover ½ quart strawberries into quarters, leaving the last 3–5 strawberries to be used as garnish.

Assemble in layers—cake, strawberry blend, whipped cream, and quartered strawberries; then repeat.

Garnish with whole strawberries.

Don't Call It English Rødgrød med Flød

A Danish Diarist's Seduction

Hanne Winarsky

A traditional dessert from Denmark, this is a cold strawberry and rhubarb soup (and you can vary it by adding all sorts of sweet summer berries). It's easy and keeps really well in the fridge for a few days. Serve as a delicious cold dessert to cool down on hot summer nights!

about 6–8 rhubarb stalks
water, as directed
2 packages frozen, sliced strawberries in syrup
3 tablespoons sugar, or to taste
3–4 tablespoons cornstarch
heavy cream (or half-and-half), for serving
sugar to taste

Take frozen strawberries out of their packages and put into a bowl on the counter to defrost, partially.

Dice rhubarb into ½-inch pieces. Put into a large pot. Add just enough water to cover the bottom of the pot (about 1 cup or so, but it depends on the pot!). Bring to a simmer. Add the rhubarb and cover; simmer over low heat. Check frequently to make sure water has not evaporated. If it has, add a little more—in very small amounts.

When rhubarb is soft (about 15 minutes or so), add strawberries and defrosted syrup from the strawberry packages. Simmer, still on low heat, until strawberries are heated and softened thoroughly (about 10 more minutes).

In a small bowl, mix 4 tablespoons of cornstarch into 2 tablespoons of water. Stir quickly until you have a smooth mixture with no lumps. Add the cornstarch and water to the simmering rhubarb and strawberry mixture. Stir thoroughly; make sure there are no lumps.

Add sugar to taste (about 3 tablespoons—depending on how much rhubarb you've used and how much syrup you've added; remember the syrup has sugar in it already). I actually prefer to keep it not super-sweet, since you will sprinkle sugar on top when serving.

Turn heat way down, and cook, stirring frequently, for about 5 more minutes, until the rhubarb and strawberry mix is about the consistency of tapioca pudding.

Remove from heat and pour into bowl to cool. Refrigerate.

Serve chilled with heavy cream or half-and-half drizzled on top, and sprinkle with sugar.

Cooking time: about 40 minutes.
Serves 6–8.

Text and Context in Apple Tarte Tatin

Pamela Schnitter

A cast-iron skillet works best when making this tart because it helps the fruit to caramelize, but any heavy-duty nonstick pan with an ovenproof handle will do.

6–8 large, firm sweet apples, such as Pippin, Northern Spy, Winesap, Granny Smith, Golden Delicious, or Mutsu, peeled and halved
1–2 lemons, halved
1 cup sugar
4 tablespoons unsalted butter
1 sheet frozen puff pastry (standard package, 17¼ ounces), thawed
all-purpose flour, for dusting

Preheat oven to 400 degrees (F).

Core apples using a melon-baller, to retain the rounded shape of the apples. Rub apples with sliced lemons to prevent browning. Set aside.

Over medium heat in a 10-inch cast-iron skillet, heat sugar and ¼ cup water. Cook until it turns a rich golden color, swirling occasionally, about 6–7 minutes.

Meanwhile, roll out puff pastry on a lightly floured surface, in one direction, to make a 14-inch circle, about ⅛-inch thick. Brush off any excess flour with a pastry brush.

Add butter to skillet. Once melted, add apples, rounded sides down, fitting as many into the skillet as possible; sauté until lightly browned.

Remove from heat, and top apples with puff pastry. Fold pastry edges under, and crimp slightly. Make two to three small cuts in puff pastry to allow the steam to escape.

Place in oven for 10 minutes. Reduce heat to 375 degrees, and bake until pastry is golden brown, about 20–25 minutes.

Remove from oven, and let cool about 2 minutes. Loosen edges with a knife.

Carefully place a plate over the skillet and flip the contents, inverting the tarte tatin.

Serve warm or at room temperature.

Serves 8.

Behind Deep Blue

Building the World-Champion Coffee Cake Mary Lynn McCarthy

From Duxbury High School.

Crumb topping
¼ cup firm margarine (½ stick)
½ cup sugar
1 cup all-purpose flour
½ teaspoon cinnamon

Cake
2 cups flour
¾ cup sugar
¾ cup milk
2½ teaspoons baking powder
¾ teaspoon salt
2 cups blueberries (if frozen, first thaw and drain)

Glaze
½ cup confectionary sugar
¼ teaspoon vanilla extract
1½–2 teaspoons hot water

Preheat oven to 375 degrees (F), and grease round pan (9 inches across and 1½ inches deep) or square pan (8 x 8 x 2 inches).

Crumb topping

Cut margarine into all other ingredients with fork or pastry blender.

Cake

Mix all ingredients, except berries; beat 30 seconds. Fold in berries. Spread cake batter into pan and sprinkle with topping. Bake for 45 minutes, or until toothpick comes out clean.

Glaze

Combine confectionary sugar and vanilla extract; drizzle hot water over mixture until smooth. Drizzle glaze over warm cake.

Serves 6.

A Farewell to Waists White Chocolate Bread Pudding

Sharyn Zasada

A recipe from my niece, Chef Marianne Cueno-Powell, at A Little Café, Voorhees, N.J.

12 croissants
1–1½ quarts heavy cream
9 eggs
1 cup white sugar
2 tablespoons vanilla extract
2 vanilla beans
2 tablespoons good white chocolate (Valarona)

Preheat oven to 375 degrees (F).

Prepare fresh vanilla from beans: slice pod open and scrape fresh vanilla out with knife. Cut croissants into slices and place in 9 x 12-inch pan (greased or sprayed); set aside. In a saucepan, heat heavy cream, adding white chocolate and vanilla extract, until chocolate melts; set aside. In a bowl, whisk eggs, white sugar, and fresh vanilla (from beans). Fold egg mixture slowly into warm cream and chocolate mix. Pour mixture over croissants in 9 x 12–inch pan and bake in oven 35–40 minutes, until set.

Serve slightly warm, with raspberry and mango purée and topped with pieces of shaved white chocolate.

The Music of a Distant Fudge Cake

Optimization for Pudding Manifolds

Chuck Creesy and Gretchen Oberfranc

We believe that the source for this recipe is the Chicago Tribune. *Gretchen's family has been making the Fudge Pudding Cake since the late 1960s.*

Cake
1 cup flour
⅔ cup sugar
2 teaspoons baking powder
2 tablespoons cocoa
1 teaspoon salt
½ cup milk
1 teaspoon vanilla extract
2 tablespoons melted butter
½ cup chopped nuts

Topping
1 cup brown sugar
¼ cup cocoa
1½ cups boiling water

Preheat oven to 350 degrees (F).

Sift together 3 times: flour, sugar, baking powder, cocoa, and salt. Combine milk, vanilla extract, and melted butter. Combine liquid and dry ingredients; beat until smooth. Stir in ½ cup chopped nuts. Spread in a buttered 6-cup casserole dish. Mix brown sugar with ¼ cup cocoa; sprinkle over the batter. Pour 1½ cups boiling water over the entire cake. Bake for 50 minutes.

Serve with ice cream or whipped cream.

Direct Mail Cherry Coffee Cake

Leslie Nangle

Topping
1 tablespoon cinnamon
½ cup brown sugar
2 tablespoons butter
2 tablespoons flour
½ cup finely chopped nuts

Filling
1 can cherry pie filling

Batter
½ pound butter, softened
2 teaspoons baking soda
1½ cups sugar
2 teaspoons baking powder
2 eggs
3⅔ cups flour
16 ounces sour cream
2 teaspoons vanilla extract

Preheat oven to 350 degrees (F).

For batter, combine all dry batter ingredients, and then add all wet ingredients. Mix together. Batter will be thick. Grease a 9 x 13-inch baking pan. Pour in half the batter. Spread on the pie filling. Pour remaining batter on top. Mix together the topping ingredients, and sprinkle over the cake. Bake for about 1 hour (or longer—you'll need to monitor, depending on your oven).

You'll get a great response rate, repeat customers, and maybe high cholesterol.

Grandma's Cinnamon Flop

The Complete Annotated Edition Martha Camp

BATTER
1 cup white sugar
¼ cup shortening
2 cups flour (all white, or half white and half wheat)
1 teaspoon baking powder
1 teaspoon baking soda
1 teaspoon vanilla extract
1 egg
¾ cup sour whole milk, or buttermilk

TOPPING
3 teaspoons cinnamon
2 tablespoons flour
¼ cup butter
½ cup brown sugar

BATTER

Preheat oven to 375 degrees (F).

Grease an 8-inch square pan, or double the recipe and use a 9 x 13-inch pan. Place egg in 1-cup measure; fill cup with sour milk or buttermilk. (To make sour milk, add 1 teaspoon vinegar to ¾ cup whole milk and set aside for 10 minutes.)

Cream shortening and sugar together. Add, alternately, dry ingredients and egg-milk mixture (plus vanilla extract). Spread batter in pan.

TOPPING

Mix all ingredients to crumb stage; spread over batter. Use more around edges of the batter, since it bakes toward the center. Push topping lightly into batter over the entire surface.

Bake for 40–45 minutes.

Fruit topping variation: Slice apples or peaches; press firmly into batter, and then sprinkle sparingly with sugar and cinnamon.

Grandma's Cinnamon Flop

Martha Camp

The Complete Annotated Edition

"Flop" as verb (intransitive)

1. To fall or plump down suddenly, esp. with noise; drop or turn with a sudden bump or thud (sometimes followed by *down*): *The puppy flopped down on the couch.*
2. To change suddenly, as from one side or party to another (often followed by over).
3. To be a complete failure; fail: *The play flopped dismally.*
4. (*informal*) To sleep or be lodged: *To flop at a friend's house.*
5. To swing loosely; bounce; flap: *His long hair flops in his eyes when he runs.*

"Flop" as verb (transitive)

6. To drop with a sudden bump or thud: *He flopped his books on a chair.*
7. To dispose (oneself) in a heavily negligent manner: *to flop oneself in a chair.*
8. To invert (as the negative of a photograph) so that the right and left sides are transposed.

"Flop" as noun

9. The act of flopping.
10. The sound of flopping; a thud.
11. A failure: *The new comedy was a flop.*
12. (*Informal*) A place to sleep; temporary lodging: *The mission offered a flop and a free breakfast.*

"Flop" in coffee cake

13. Kitchen physics that predicts the sinking of the topping into the batter during baking.
14. Opportunity for one's spouse to make jokes such as "Here, have some of my wife's flop."

Heroic Cocoa Brownies with a Thousand Calories

Terri O'Prey

A classic, updated with a dark chocolate twist, and expanded with a rich frosting.

BROWNIES
soft butter, for greasing pan
flour, for dusting buttered pan
4 large eggs
2 cups brown sugar
8 ounces melted butter
1¼ cups dark cocoa, sifted
2 teaspoons vanilla extract
½ cup flour, sifted
½ teaspoon kosher salt

GANACHE FROSTING
1 cup heavy cream
12 ounces dark chocolate chips

BROWNIES

Preheat oven to 300 degrees (F). Butter and flour an 8-inch square pan.

In a mixer fitted with whisk attachment, beat eggs at medium speed until fluffy and light. Add sugar. Add remaining ingredients, and mix to combine. Pour batter into greased and floured pan and bake for 45 minutes (a toothpick inserted into the center of the pan should come out clean). Remove pan to a rack to cool; prepare frosting (below).

GANACHE FROSTING

Bring cream to boil in a small saucepan or double boiler. Remove from heat and add chocolate. Stir until most of the chocolate is melted. Cover and let stand for 10 minutes. Gently stir or whisk until completely smooth. Pour over cooling brownies.

Cool completely or refrigerate before serving. Results in a dark, heavy brownie, best enjoyed in small servings. Recipe serves 8–12 (depending on the appetite for sinfully rich tidbits), and easily doubles for larger crowds.

Cognitive Theory of Microwave Apple Crisp

Leslie Grundfest

From Elizabeth Siboldi's high school cooking class; the best part of this recipe is that it is made in the microwave and frees up the oven for storage.

5 cups apples
6 tablespoons butter
¾ cup packed brown sugar
¾ cup quick cooking oats
⅓ cup raisins and/or dried cranberries
⅓ cup chopped walnuts
1 teaspoon cinnamon

Peel, core, and slice apples. Place apples in an 8-inch microwave-safe baking dish. Sprinkle cranberries, raisins, and walnuts over apples. In a separate bowl, melt butter in microwave. Combine melted butter, brown sugar, oats, and cinnamon—until crumbly; sprinkle mixture over apples evenly. Microwave on high for 5 minutes. Turn dish and microwave for another 5 minutes.

Serve warm with vanilla ice cream.

Through a Crème Brûlée That Shines

Donna Goetz

2 cups whipping cream
2½ cups half-and-half
7–8 tablespoons white sugar
8 egg yolks
1 tablespoon real vanilla extract
¾ cup light brown sugar
2 tablespoons fresh lemon zest

Preheat oven to 300 degrees (F).

Heat cream in double boiler; the water should be boiling. Stir in the white sugar so that it melts into the hot cream. In a separate bowl, beat egg yolks until light. Pour hot cream over them gradually, stirring vigorously; stir in the vanilla extract. Set 10 custard cups (ovenproof) in large pan filled with 1 inch of boiling water. Sprinkle the bottom of each cup with the lemon zest—just enough to cover the bottom; fill cups ¾-full with cream mixture. Bake until an inserted knife comes out clean; this takes 45 minutes to 1 hour. Remove the custard from the hot water. Chill thoroughly, at least 4 hours.

Note: Crème Brûlée can be prepared the day before, up to this point.

Five minutes before serving, cover the surface with the brown sugar. Gently pat it down to create a layer. Set the cups in a pan filled with cracked ice and a little cold water. Put the crème under the broiler until the sugar turns dark brown.

Serve immediately. Refrigerate any leftovers. The burnt sugar liquefies to become a delicious sauce on the crème.

The "No Bullshit"/"No Flour" Chocolate Whisky Torte

Ian Malcolm

TORTE
½ pound unsalted butter
½ pound semisweet chocolate
1½ cups toasted pecans, chopped
1 cup cocoa
1½ cups sugar
6 eggs, at room temperature
¾ cup Scotch whisky

GLAZE
½ pound semisweet chocolate
1 tablespoon unsalted butter
1 cup toasted pecans, chopped

TORTE

Preheat oven to 350 degrees (F).

Melt butter with chocolate; set aside. In mixer, combine pecans, cocoa, and sugar. Add eggs; mix until smooth. Pour in melted chocolate and butter. Add whisky; do not whip. Pour into 9-inch springform pan lined with parchment or waxed paper. Bake in oven for 1 hour while reading a philosophy monograph. Cool and cover with glaze (below).

GLAZE

Melt chocolate and butter over a bain-marie;* let cool until chocolate begins to thicken. Spread chocolate over and around sides of cake. Press the pecans into the sides of the cake.

*For those without a fully equipped alchemical workshop in the basement, a double boiler may be substituted for the traditional bain-marie—*pace Maria Hebraea*.

A Digression

Four-Footed Amity

Biscuits for Millie

Jennifer Formichelli

When I think about cooking, I realize that I enjoy it for the same reasons that I love literature: cooking creates company. Good food, praised equally by Dr. Johnson and T. S. Eliot, becomes an occasion for the best conversation—table talk. How many memorable evenings occur around the dinner table, with wine, food, friends, laughter, and the conversations that bind and hold us together?

This recipe, however, is dedicated to another breed of company. Besides literature, there is no better companionship than the friendship of dogs. It is unique in its interkindness, a company based on the perfect amity of silence. Dogs, in their expressiveness, have found that place where all words go eventually: where, as Eliot puts it, "Words, after speech, reach / Into the silence." And dogs by nature love food; it is only by grace that they love us.

My dog Millicent was diagnosed with chronic renal failure (CRF) in January 2006. Rather than despair, I did what dogs like best: I cooked food. This is a recipe for a kidney-friendly, low-protein, low-phosphorus dog biscuit, beloved by Millie.

2½–3 cups white rice flour (organic, if possible)
1 egg white
6 tablespoons organic reduced-sodium chicken broth (no more than 3 grams protein allowed per serving, if you are cooking for a CRF dog)
1 tablespoon garlic powder (no salt added)
¼ cup cooked chicken
3 teaspoons water
1 tablespoon dolomite powder (optional; for CRF dogs, it works as a phosphorus binder, while helping to make biscuits crunchy)
1 head cauliflower, broken into florets
2 cups carrots, either baby carrots or diced
2 cups spinach
1 teaspoon butter

Preheat oven to 350 degrees (F).

First, cook the cauliflower, carrots, and spinach in unsalted water until quite soft. Mash and put aside. Put the chicken, chicken broth, and water into a blender and blend to a purée. Set aside. Melt butter in microwave. Set aside.

In a large bowl, combine rice flour, garlic powder, dolomite powder, and egg white. Add melted butter. Add chicken purée and stir. Add vegetable mash until you have a sufficiently soft consistency to have absorbed all the flour.

Shape biscuits—usually about 1½–2 cups of mash for each. (These will be softer and more watery than wheat-flour–based biscuits; you may also form them into balls or patties. I make mine about the size of a 50-cent piece, or twice the size of a quarter.)

Put biscuits onto a nonstick cooking sheet. They do not rise, so you can put them together closely, but make sure they don't touch. Bake in oven for 1 hour. Check to test for crispness. One hour gives you a moist biscuit; 2 hours (check to be sure you don't burn them) gives you a very crisp biscuit (Millie prefers these). Be careful not to burn: I find my dogs are snooty about burned biscuits.

If you make them crispy, you can crumble them to make tasty training treats that are low-fat, low-salt, and healthy.

This recipe makes about 75 biscuits—a week's supply for two.

HUGHES
FAMILY SCALE

Appendixes

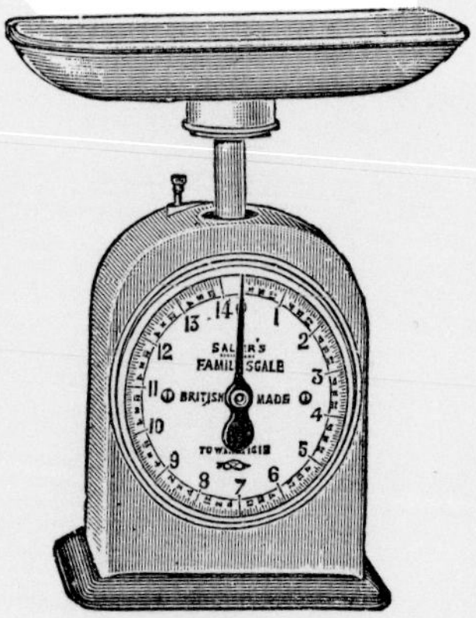

Measurement Conversions

500 AAs = 12 steps

250 archaeologists = 1 printrun

1 castoff = 3 fluid page counts

7 dry quarts page counts = 1 Heisenberg

4 exclamation points = 1 blurb!!!!

1 gross margin = 2 extra belt notches

4 nonexclusive permission grants = 1 barroom disturbance

12 point leading = 1 FDA ban

1st proofs = 4 shot glasses

1 quarto = 2 pintos

1 ragged right margin = 2008 electoral college

running heads = always double the quantity of running heads to obtain the correct amount of calculating feet

1 signature = 32 contract addendums

Glossary of Terms Shared by Cookery & Publishing

(For Example, This Is an Appendix)

Binding: What an egg does for meatloaf.
Binding: The sewn, notched, or paste-based collation of a book's signatures.

Clarify: A treatment of butter or broth to render it clear, pure, and pellucid.
Clarify: What editors perpetrate upon authors' words.

Dash: A problematically informal expression of dry measurement, indicative of something between a Nip and a Mess.
Dash: Typographical symbols of varying lengths: the en dash and the em dash, which correspond to the widths of the capital letters N and M respectively.

Dessert: A course served after a meal, usually pastry, cake, pudding, or fruit-based.
Dissert: To speak or write at length on a subject.

Extract: A liquid that contains the essence of a flavor, such as vanilla or almond. Often spirituous.
Extract: A passage that is politely lifted from another source and added, with appropriate incantations of indebtedness, into one's own text.

Fiber: Something that makes food healthier. Paper is very high in fiber and fat-free, but we do not recommend eating it.
Fiber: Paper is made most often from plant fiber such as wood, cotton, or linen.

Mature: What happens to wines and cheeses as they sit around in the warehouse.
Mature: An optimistic term applied to backlist titles. The payoff can be great (as when classic titles by Einstein, Popper, or Rorty become essential undergraduate reading); when the process fails, the matured books are left out on the curbside for pickup by our friends at Guaranteed Destruction Associates of Bayonne, New Jersey.

Paste: A mixture of flour and water, the basis for pasta and pastry.
Paste: The classic archival glue used for centuries in the production of books is wheat paste—a product of combining wheat starch and water.

Ps and Qs: Pints and quarts.

Ps and Qs: In the Golden Age of Hot Type, these two letters were commonly confused because the lowercase letters are mirror images of each other.

Proof: The desired consequence of the pudding.

Proof: A preliminary test run of typeset copy.

Pulp: In fruits, the good stuff.

Pulp: The stuff paper is made from; *alt.*, the stuff that less-than-scholarly books are made from.

Table: A piece of furniture commonly used for dining.

Table: The typeset display of related facts or figures, in rows and columns.

Table: When the Editorial Board suggests that your hot-shot author's new manuscript be consigned to the "Fix It or Forget It" pile.

Index

THE END